Always With You

To my dear
brother Tim
with all the love
& affection
May God bless
You
Pastor James A. Doss
Sept 18/2010

Always With You

James A. Doss

To order additional copies of this book, contact:
Xlibris Corporation
1-888-795-4274
www.Xlibris.com
Orders@Xlibris.com
79354

Contents

I dedicate this book to my LORD and Savior JESUS CHRIST.

To my wife Hui Juan Ma with whom I have shared many an adventure. I will always be grateful for all the love and affection and care you have shown me. With my deepest gratitude and sincere appreciation for all that GOD has made you to be and all that you have accomplished I will always remain your ever loving and ever proud husband. I know that our LORD and SAVIOR JESUS CHRIST will continue to bless our life's journey and may HE be continually glorified in our lives.

To my dearest daughter Anjali, you are an incredible blessing to my life, you made me a father and I am ever so grateful for the richness of that experience. I saw you come into this world and I've seen you grow in leaps and bounds. GOD Almighty has blessed you with a strong mind and a caring heart. You are going to achieve so much more in your life than I ever have and LORD willing I will be around to see them all. No matter where the road of life takes you I want you to remember this, not religion, not ritual, not tradition, not denomination but relationship, relationship with your LORD and SAVIOR JESUS CHRIST. Keep JESUS in the focus of your life and you will experience what an amazing blessing that will be and more than me or anyone else of this world JESUS will be always with you.

With all my Love

Dad

To my Loving Daughter Veena,

You have brought out the kid in me and I have always loved to see you grow and become a strong individual. You have a heart of Gold Veena and you have repeatedly allowed me to see the kinder more caring side of you. GOD will bless you for all the kindness you have shown your dad. I bless you with all the blessing a father can give his daughter. I am grateful for your sincerity and honesty. Continue to keep the faith you have in our LORD and SAVIOR the LORD JESUS CHRIST. HIS promise and guarantee to you is this, And Lo I will be with you always even unto the end of this age. And if anyone can keep his promise the LORD JESUS can. Live, be blessed and be a blessing.

I will always be Your ever loving Dad.

I want to personally extend my heartfelt gratitude to

Pastor David Machado, Pastor Wilbes Mbiya, Pastor Kayode Morakinyo, Pastor Abbe Adenuga, Pastor Kevin Streahl, Deaconess Dorthy Dowty, Deaconess Setiawati Rahardjo, Jessica Acosta, Jodi Gaylord, Ron Brown, Edie Brown, David Hewitt, Jeanniee Hewitt, Roxy Runsthrough, Wylie Runsthrough, Corie Cassel, Trinity Cassel and Oliver Cassel Angie Molinari, Rick Molinari, Lyla Peterson, Ona Morakinyo, Ebun Morakinyo, Dara Morakinyo, Daren and Heather Late Pastor Dana Haynes, Stephen Haynes, Floydean, Patience Mbiya, Kudzai and Alec Sithole, William, Peter Alexander, Jenny and Morrigan, Durkins, Angelie Kebede, Jakey Trinh, Brian, Cheryl Miller, May and Owen Miller, Mike and Marty, James, Cindy Pastor Nang and Kim and Lydia Nguyen, Bradley Clark, Paula Noya, Gerd Noya, Pastor Johann Kusnadi, Pat and Joyce, Daniel, Tatsuko, Victoria, Pastor Steve Bilkstad, Abraham , Tony Vic Jim Estes, Debbie Estes, ana Alicia, Catherine, Bear, Pastor Rene and Evie Sahir, Pastor Billy and Marnet, TJ and Faith, Wawan Seputro, Bryan Waddell, Jim Kjelgaard, Asoporo Okembo, Bob and Colleen Harvey, Mike, Suzanne Ma, Alex and Benny Ma, Kristy, Evan and Gloria Otteson, Kevin Otteson, G.

And a very special thanks to my Mother in law and Father in law
Kai Leung Ma and Yan Lan Chen

To My Dearest Mom and Dad, to whom I owe my deepest and most sincerest gratitude.
K.P.V. Ramani

My name is James let me tell you about JESUS

Chapter 1

Always with You

And Lo I will be with you always, even until the end
of this age.

—Matthew 28:20

JESUS's words echo through the ages, as a constant reminder
to each and every one of us who has boldly stepped onto
this journey of faith and ventured into the uncharted realms of
individual reality. Throughout the many centuries, countless
people groups—whether rich or poor, great or small, men or
women, children or adults, irrespective of their color, creed, race,

or language—have so abundantly held on to this promise as a sole means of their personal sustenance. And time and again this guarantee, this personal promise has made it possible for those countless, to not just survive in life but to thrive in it, against insurmountable odds and against formidable foes.

HIS word is strong, HIS word is true, HIS word is alive, and above all it is sufficient to meet your every need. If ever you needed an affirmation, if you ever needed an encouragement or a shoulder to cry on, you can find the strength you need in HIS precious words. Allow me to delineate in the ensuing chapters the strength and the power and the influence HIS words can have on life as we know it.

Madras, India, geographically classified as a semiarid desert, now has become the home to over 4.6 million people. The density of population in Madras far surpasses any individual city within the continental United States. I grew up in a Catholic family in this semiarid desert, with what little resources a middle-income family could then afford.

I attended the Catholic Mass as religiously as I could (no pun intended). A lot of growing up happened between my search for time and resources and my quest for GOD. During those growing-up years, I learned that riches along with everything else come and go and the only real anchor anyone really has is their loving relationship with GOD Almighty. Now this is hard to figure out; some take a lifetime to do this, and some (to my utter dismay) never really do? I always looked up to GOD to be my anchor. I cannot say (even now) that I fully understand or fully grasp the concept and the depth of a personal relationship with the maker of the universe, but you know my understanding has changed and so has my faith, and I am completely convinced that this is a tailor-made journey (of faith) for each one of us. No one's experience and walk is the same as the other, yet there are always some common elements that seem to draw us closer to one another and therein allow us to see in each of us the indwelling of the Almighty.

During those growing-up years in Madras, India, I often found myself in need of resources—resources of all kinds—and I could never tell you exactly how or when something was going to happen. But even at that early age, I could see a pattern for my life as to how the Almighty provides.

Whatever it was that I needed, I always found myself at the right place and at the right time. The right people seemed to pop out of nowhere. In all this I must confess that GOD gave me the opportunity to either choose (by faith) that it was indeed the providential hand of GOD at work in my life or to simply attribute these things to coincidence and the chance factor or mere luck.

I hope you can see through my eyes and possibly through the rest of this book that when you choose faith, what was once hazy and muddled and unclear now becomes precise and neat and clear. HIS loving hands can be seen ever so carefully and meticulously, working behind the tapestry of one's life.

In HIM all the promises of GOD remain a veritable yes. The one promise and guarantee that I so overwhelmingly hold on to is the one declared by JESUS before his final departure:

And Lo I will be with you always, even until the end of this age.

This and this alone is reason enough to get up each morning and face whatever life may throw your way.

God bless you richly in Christ Jesus.

Amen.

Chapter 2

Always with Me

I pastor a nondenominational church in Portland, Oregon (Calvary Bible Church) and I have been a pastor there for almost eight years now. Before I had the privilege to pastor this church, I had the opportunity to work with an inner-city ministry, also in Portland, Oregon, for a period of seven years.

During these years of ministry, I have had the privilege of having seen GOD at work in the lives of many individuals. And what a privilege it has been to have had those shared memories. In part this book is the result of the rich input that they have had on my life. In a manner of speaking, I dedicate this book to the influence and experience they have contributed both individually and collectively to my spiritual growth.

Whether you are in ministry or not, it is good to be reminded of how GOD is always at work in the life of a believer. It is good to see how GOD is so meticulously and thoroughly orchestrating the events of a Christian's life with a precision that far surpasses any human profession or endeavor. And in this book I want to share with you the life stories of such individuals whom GOD has made memorable and in whose lives I have seen and witnessed the hand of the Almighty at work.

It is my hope that you can relate to their lives as you continue your own faith journey, all the while experiencing his presence and his faithfulness in your life. If life is to be enjoyed, there is only one way to do it—it is by having the knowledge that the hand of the Almighty is at work in your life and that he has promised to be there for you all the way to the end.

So hold on and enjoy the journey for he has promised,

*And Lo I will be with you always, even until the end of this age.

Amen.

Chapter 3

Is It Time

GOD made a visit to Abraham when he was in his nineties and made him a promise; the depth of that promise can be seen in Genesis 17:5-6:

> Vv5 "I AM changing your name from Abram to Abraham, because I Am making you a father of many nations." vv6 "I will give you many descendants, new nations will be born from you, and kings will come from you."

The kind of promise GOD makes causes Abraham to laugh. You can observe this in Genesis 17:17:

> Abraham bowed face down on the ground and laughed and he said to himself, "Can a man have a child when he is a hundred years old? Can Sarah give birth when she is ninety?"

And Abraham suggests an alternate route to this blessing, as can be seen in Genesis 17:18:

> Then Abraham said to GOD, "Please let Ishmael be the son you promised."

Here's a simple observation that helped me a lot in life. You see in Abraham's eyes, life, as he knew it, was over or was coming to an end. He didn't consider himself to be in his prime; his prime time, according to him, was up. He had already reached a retired state of mind; he'd already called it quits. He doesn't have any major family to speak of, except an old lady (albeit stunningly beautiful for her age). If anything Abraham's been there, done that. Abraham in his lifetime had fought great battles and defended his nephew Lot. He has listened to the voice of GOD and taken off to a far and distant land. He knows from firsthand experience what living on the edge means. He hasn't had a glorious life but a GOD-fearing life, but now it seems like he believes that his time is up. (Human reasoning will always do that to you.) He understands that GOD can do anything, but pragmatism tells him that the times for accomplishing great things are up. He's not a little kid anymore, he is old, he cannot have any children, let alone becoming the father of many nations.

Can GOD really do this? The answer to you and me is yes. GOD can and will do anything that is needed to accomplish HIS will and purpose. But come on! "Let's get real here," say the many unbelieving. History tells us that GOD did get real and accomplish everything HE set out to do, in anyone's and everyone's life.

And the same GOD through HIS son JESUS CHRIST makes this promise—which I consider is the promise of all promises, the guarantee of all guarantees—and we have a choice today, whether to be like Abram (who wondered, at first) or to choose to take HIM at HIS word and allow that promise to take preeminence in our lives. That promise that you and I can so veritably hold on to is this:

And Lo I will be with you always, even until the end of this age.

Amen.

Chapter 4

Always at the Right Place

The year 2009 has been marked with several tragedies—the never-ending crisis in Iraq, the Taliban's consistent and concerted efforts at causing some sort of harm, the global financial crisis, record-high foreclosures, unemployment figures in double digits, stock markets taking a daily plunge and exploring new levels at the bottom—and no matter what cross section of the economy one takes the time to analyze, it seems like everyone and everything has been adversely affected in one way or another.

Here I am writing a book to encourage you with a promise from CHRIST saying, "Lo I will always be with you." How do we interpret that in the light of where we find ourselves today? What seems to be the hermeneutics behind this biblical quote, a direct verbatim from Christ JESUS? (Incidentally, neither is Christ his last name nor is the whole name an expletive; I never did quite understand how that got worked into an explanation for tough situations. Do some research on it, when you find some time, in the interim.)

The other day I was in a store, and the lady in front of me was buying a cola of some sort, and then she was frantically digging through the contents of her purse in order to find the right change. From the looks of it, it seemed like she was in abject penury. I waited and observed another lady (who was standing behind me up unto this point) slowly ease her way to the front and tap the cola-buying lady on her shoulder, and offered to buy her the cola. She also added, "Go get yourself whatever else you need. I gotch ya." It was the end of the month, a time when cash flow was as good as the campaign promises. (I have no specific party inclination, but generally speaking, most politicians seem to promise more—way more than they can deliver.) But that sweet innocent generosity—to see someone step forward and bless another person's life—is nothing short of "divine."

Yet, on another occasion, I had the chance to observe this man who was at the checkout at this major department store; and to my utter dismay, when he reached the counter, he pulled out a small bag full of Lincoln pennies. He had a cold sandwich on the counter, just one, and he said that he had been to at least three different stores and nobody would take it and he desperately needed to eat something. The clerk appeared to be in no mood to accommodate the painstaking process of accepting payments for the merchandise in pennies. It took several awkward moments; nevertheless, the clerk seemed to have managed to communicate the store policies to this patron. It was rather awkward because the man appeared to be very sincere and very apologetic all at the same time. He wasn't pulling a prank, and there were no hidden cameras watching to observe the fun of unloading a bagful of pennies on an unsuspecting store clerk.

All of a sudden there appeared this man; he may have come from somewhere in the back of the line (it didn't really matter), but he was there. As the man of the hour, he stepped up and offered to buy that patron his merchandise. The patron behaved in an even more dignified way and offered the man his bag of pennies in return for the merchandise. The man took the patron's bag of pennies and shook hands with him and left, leaving the patron with his merchandise and his dignity intact.

It seemed like nothing much. You probably have witnessed something like this before. Maybe you were even on the giving end of this transaction with the patron on the receiving end, or you may have had firsthand experience of being in the exact same shoes as the patron with the pennies. Whatever the case may be, all I want you to consider is the simple fact that timing in both these instances was amazingly perfect. Someone in need found their help by someone who "happened" to come by.

There are countless stories, both from personal experiences and the vicarious shared experiences of friends concerning the miraculous interference of strangers who seem to somehow show up at the right time and the right place.

In the book of Acts 8:26-39, the text reads as follows in the New International Version:

26 Now an angel of the Lord said to Philip, "Go south to the road—the desert road—that goes down from Jerusalem to Gaza." 27 So he started out, and on his way he met an Ethiopian eunuch, an important official in charge of all the treasury of Candace, queen of the Ethiopians. This man had gone to Jerusalem to worship, 28 and on his way home was sitting in his chariot reading the book of Isaiah the prophet. 29 The Spirit told Philip, "Go to that chariot and stay near it."

30 Then Philip ran up to the chariot and heard the man reading Isaiah the prophet. "Do you understand what you are reading?" Philip asked.

31 "How can I," he said, "unless someone explains it to me?" So he invited Philip to come up and sit with him.

32 The eunuch was reading this passage of Scripture: 32 "He was led like a sheep to the slaughter, 32 and as a lamb before the shearer is silent, 32 so he did not open his mouth.

33 In his humiliation he was deprived of justice. 33 Who can speak of his descendants? 33 For his life was taken from the earth."

34 The eunuch asked Philip, "Tell me, please, who is the prophet talking about, himself or someone else?" 35 Then Philip began with that very passage of Scripture and told him the good news about Jesus.

36 As they traveled along the road, the3y came to some water and the eunuch said, "Look, here is water. Why shouldn't I be baptized?" 38 And he gave orders to stop the chariot. Then both Philip and the eunuch went down into the water and Philip baptized him. 39 When they came up out of the water, the Spirit of the Lord suddenly took Philip away, and the eunuch did not see him again, but went on his way rejoicing.

This story is fascinating, and it offers a rare glimpse of the divine interference. Here was this Ethiopian eunuch whom nobody had heard about up until this point, and couple that with the fact that Philip had no idea about the existence of the Ethiopian eunuch makes it all the more fascinating.

GOD ALMIGHTY in his omniscience carefully and meticulously orchestrates this event in history. It shows that among several other things, the GOD of the universe is a caring GOD and the salvation of his people is important to HIM, even if it is only one lonely soul out in the middle of nowhere. HE is still willing and able to bend heaven and earth to reach that one soul. You may be the one in need, and I want you to know that you are not forgotten or written of or uncared for. *Wherever or whatever situation* you find yourself in, have the utmost confidence to choose to believe that your creator has not and will not leave you alone. HE cares deeply for you, and even as you read this, he has a divinely orchestrated plan for your life. Not even a grain of sand on the seashore is erratically misplaced, but rather exquisitely and delicately positioned one grain of sand over the other thereby establishing perfect symmetry and order. If GOD can care enough to go over (what may seem like) the small details of life so exquisitely, how much more do you think does he care about your life and your well-being. The answer is more than you'll ever know.

If this sounds too far-fetched or if it sounds too verbose or ostentatious without much meaning or substance, I assure you that it is a legitimate concern that you may have. And if you are wondering why I would agree with you, here is why? Well, allow me to expound. You see the primary ingredient for anyone to experience the goodness of GOD in all its fullness is for them to first of all experience faith. And that isn't that difficult thing after all. Let's pause for a moment and evaluate any one of your meaningful relationships, be it your spouse, your child, your parent, your siblings, your uncle, your aunt, or your distant cousin, whoever that may be. Now when you come to the position in your relationship where you can define that relationship as a meaningful or a significant one, then you can understand or identify with what I am about to say. You see in that relationship, for it to be either meaningful or significant, you must have learned to have a pattern of established trust. Now this pattern of trust slowly becomes so pervasive that when the person is physically not present, he or she elicits the same amount of trust from you. If you say, "No, they don't," you're either saying that just to refute an argument or you are yet to experience a significant or meaningful relationship. Let's assume you have experienced a significant and a meaningful relationship with someone and therefore have a reasonable understanding of trust. That trusting relationship is in a way uniquely analogous to a trusting relationship with GOD. For this I am drawing an inference from what is known to what is unknown. This, in many ways, is similar to faith. You see if GOD was present in person, it would not take a whole lot of faith for you to believe in him. HIS physical absence or, as I call it, his optical absence is what is causing many to question the different attributes of GOD. But if you learn to lay aside those presuppositions and build on the foundation of a simple trust, then you can begin to get somewhere in establishing a loving and trusting relationship with the unseen GOD Almighty. This in turn causes a chain reaction, and from this point onward, every aspect of life begins to shine as if invigorated by a new force of energy and one begins to see the work of the Almighty supernaturally guiding and leading, carefully and meticulously through the ups and downs and treacherous quagmires of life. And people long for that sort of a spiritual high, a nirvana if you will. A state of mind, when you no longer need any more substantiation, whatsoever, of the existence and presence of GOD Almighty revealed through HIS son JESUS CHRIST. That very knowledge that there is a GOD who is in control, that there is a GOD who is in charge causes a wellspring of hope to arise in you. The outpouring of that wellspring is what we call faith, and this causes many doors and windows of opportunities come your way; and life, as you know it, will never be the same again.

And here is the bonus; it is indeed the mother of all bonuses, and this is it. The faith journey that you've begun is never a lonely journey or a journey of solitude. You see, the GOD you've come to put your faith in isn't just a GOD who is out there or even a

GOD who is just here; but rather, HE is GOD incarnate, the God of all gods, and the LORD of all lords. HE is the CHRIST, and HE is JESUS, and HE boldly declares as a promise for all time:

And Lo I will be with you always, even until the end of this age.

Chapter 5

On Your Side

Adrian Clark, a retired medical doctor from Madras, India, and an Indian American man who grew up in the suburbs of Madras, also known in India as Chennai, lost his father to "waywardness" (as he put it).By the time he was ten years old, Adrian came to the quick realization that he had to fight for attention, money, instruction, and affection (and whatever else a ten-year-old would need in Madras, India) all at the same time although not necessarily in that order.

I write about him because, as a retired medical doctor and as a retired adult, he vividly recalls a tragic life experience of his. He remembers the day, the date, the time, and the modality of his encounter with his biological father. He recalls his father calling on him one bright, sunny afternoon, and it goes something like this. (Keep in mind his father has not been in contact with him since he was ten. He had taken off to live his own life somewhere else and left Adrian and his mother to fend for themselves.) A fellow doctor yells, "Call for Dr. Adrian," and then someone else patches the phone call over to Dr. Adrian.

Adrian answers the phone, "Hello, this is Dr. Adrian Clark," and the voice on the other end goes, "Ahem! I am your father." (To Adrian, this wasn't his Jedi moment! None whatsoever!) "I heard you hit the lottery and bought a house and everything."

Adrian stays quiet, overwhelmed with all kinds of emotions, but his training as a seasoned medical doctor allows him to keep his cool so to speak.

And his father continues, "By the way, be nice to your fellow doctors. Don't be mean to them, like you are to me."

Adrian is now ready to take the drain hose and drench himself, to cool off the raging anger inside of him. He's got a major "what did you just say to me" moment going on.

Meanwhile, his father continues through all this great silence from Adrian's end, "You may have won the lottery, but I want you to share, like I taught you to. I thought I taught you better than this [in the matter of sharing the lottery gains among other things]." Once again his father simply continues as if he was carrying on a normal conversation with his son, not once acknowledging, "I know I left you all, and I am really sorry, etc., etc." Rather he made it sound like a "here's what I think you can do for me" conversation.

Being that Adrian had reached his max as to how much more of this he could take, Adrian quietly says, "I am at work, and I can't really talk right now," and finds a way to hang up the phone.

This conversation was bound to have its ripple effect and cause Adrian to have some serious questions about people and their value systems. And also, it was bound to have an adverse effect on any serious relationships that he might explore at a later date. Needless to say that the people, the ones he does get involved with, are bound to become unsuspecting victims of Adrian's unresolved issues. Adrian has four failed marriages and still remains a single man. Given the circumstances, it isn't difficult to assume that Adrian may not have dealt with some of his issues; only time will tell.

Here's an example of a father who gave up on his parenting responsibilities and, years later, finds his son doing well and simply marches in to usurp his parental rights. I personally believe that reconciliation at all levels is good, but I also believe that the modality of this type of reconciliation needs to be carefully thought through.

In the book of John 8:1-11, there lays a vivid story of this woman who has been caught in the act of adultery.

The story goes like this (John 8:1-11, NIV):

1 But Jesus went to the Mount of Olives. 2 At dawn he appeared again in the temple courts, where all the people gathered around him, and he sat down to teach them. 3 The teachers of the law and the Pharisees brought in a woman caught in adultery. They made her stand before the group 4 and said to Jesus, "Teacher, this woman was caught in the act of adultery. 5 In the

Law Moses commanded us to stone such women. Now what do you say?" 6 They were using this question as a trap, in order to have a basis for accusing him.

6 But Jesus bent down and started to write on the ground with his finger. 7 When they kept on questioning him, he straightened up and said to them, "If any one of you is without sin, let him be the first to throw a stone at her." 8 Again he stooped down and wrote on the ground.

9 At this, those who heard began to go away one at a time, the older ones first, until only Jesus was left, with the woman still standing there. 10 Jesus straightened up and asked her, "Woman, where are they? Has no one condemned you?"

11 "No one, sir," she said.

11 "Then neither do I condemn you," Jesus declared. "Go now and leave your life of sin."

Here in this story, we see a woman who apparently had been caught in the act of adultery brought to JESUS. (Don't ask me how! It is what they did!) And the crowd had been violently breathing down her neck; they wanted to kill her by stoning her. (Whatever happened to the guy who was involved in the act of adultery? We do not know.) All that the crowd was waiting for was for JESUS to give them the okay. If JESUS had said, "On your mark, get set, and go," there would have been a barrage of stones pinning her down until she finally died.

No one in that crowd seemed to be standing up for her that day; they wanted to stone her to death, and it was actually the legal thing to do. They haven't done it yet because they wanted to see what the all-compassionate JESUS would do. Would he forsake the Jewish law, or would he forgive the woman, or would he shirk of his compassion and walk away? What would JESUS do? (Isn't that mostly the question to all of our issues and problems?) Whatever his choice, he had a captive audience eagerly peering through the reasoning skills of the Almighty.

JESUS can be seen calmly writing something on the sand. (I always wondered what it was that he wrote.) If I put myself in her shoes, the truth of the matter is I would be guilty as charged by all counts of the tenets of the Jewish law and I would have deserved to have been killed. By JESUS's definition, most people I know including me would be guilty of adultery. What can I say! GOD made us men and women, and to this day, we remain hopelessly attracted to each other and how often do we keep challenging the boundaries of propriety and commitment. The free gift of the HOLY SPIRIT is self-control, and now, more than ever, we need to ask GOD to lavish us with an abundance of self-control.

Of all the people that I could recall knowing, on that particular day, I cannot think of anyone in the crowd who would have stood up for me (except one) and shouted out to the people, "No one here is perfect anyway" (but for JESUS). Both the believers and the nonbelievers alike often seem to make this comment in life, saying, "Oh! But GOD looks at the heart!" This is often an escape mechanism. If one really had the time to consider that phrase, it would make one realize how dreadful it is for us to go before the one to whom we must bare all. No hidden thought or agenda or motive, everything is laid open, and HE gets to be the judge.

Having said that, let me take you back to my friend Adrian Clark. You see Adrian's problems and issues started early on in life. In this I must say that Adrian lacked the nurturing that is needed to bring about a good upbringing. In Adrian's case he has and always will continue to work on the improvement of himself and is continuing to cross several hurdles in that regard. But here is the best-case scenario—a child must be raised in a loving, caring, and a nurturing home in order to help bring about any kind of a good upbringing. It is indeed pivotal to have a strong foundation, and many families inevitably leave their children at a disadvantage by not providing for them with this sort of a strong foundation. A father's role is immensely significant to the development needs of a child. Whether they be a preteen, teen, or a young adult, they all have the inherent need to acquire the much-needed life skills from their parents, in this case the father. They may improve on them later in life, but it is essential to have a strong and good foundation to start with. Adrian's father had deserted him during the much-needed early developmental years, and as such, he'd lost the myriad of opportunities he may have had at imparting life skills and life lessons to his son. This in turn has had its ripple effect in the growth and development of Adrian. Though Adrian may have developed many a coping mechanisms to overcome the hurdles of his life, there still lies the underlying void created by the lack of proper parenting. Without playing any blame game, it is important to see that unlike your earthly father, GOD incarnate in JESUS CHRIST will not abandon you or leave you or forsake you, no matter what the odds. When no one else was willing to stand up for that woman that day, JESUS did, and he still does. When you place your trust in HIM, you can see that HE will provide, HE will protect, HE will nurture, HE will save, HE will understand, HE will fulfill any and all of the deepest longings you may have, HE will fill in the greatest of the greatest of the gaping voids of your life, and HE will do it effortlessly and HE will do it consistently. HE will deliver come rain or shine, come thunderstorms or tornadoes, come recessions or depressions, come war or famine, come morning or night, come summer or winter, come good times or bad times, come destruction or disease; and even if you die, HE can and will bring you to life because he is the life and the resurrection and in HIM there is no lie, no foul, no darkness, no speck or spot. You can't hold HIM back from delivering what he has promised. HE is and always will be our ever-present help and our strong tower, and HE has made this promise to you and me:

> And Lo I will be with you always, even until the end of this age.

Amen.

Chapter 6

What Is Patience?

Sergeant Jessica Acosta, a young American girl who fought for this country, was the result of an interracial marriage between her Mexican father and an Anglican mother. Unbeknownst to most, Jessica is also an excellent Sunday school teacher. She is bright as she is beautiful and vibrant as she is disciplined all at the same time.

She lost her father at a young age and was raised in a family of six siblings and a single mom. Jessica often recalls fond memories of her dad and misses having him around in her later years.

But she remembers all the life lessons her father had taught her during his short but sweet reprieve.

Compelled by convictions, patriotism, and a strong sense of duty, Jessica joined the United States Army. She completed her basic training and was soon deployed into the thicket of operation Iraqi Freedom.

Here in the middle of all this, she met Michael, a fellow army soldier; and the two began what can only be described as an army-style courtship, talking over the enemy airwaves and texting amid army-debriefing sessions (that sort of thing so to speak). Things were beginning to look good for this couple on a personal level. And lo and behold, Michael asked for Jessica's hand in marriage, and the two were now engaged to be married. However, they decided to wait until after their deployment.

Jessica ended her deployment with flying colors and came back to her home in Portland, Oregon. Here she dedicated her life to the well-being of the children who came to her home church. In the meantime, Michael still remained deployed in Bahrain. They continued their courtship and stayed in touch via e-mail, phone calls, text messages, loving gifts, and shared memories of deployment stories.

Jessica found in Michael a good man, the kind of person GOD Almighty would want for her. Their courtship continued while Jessica remained a Sunday school teacher in Portland, Oregon. She was and still is a Sunday school teacher, and she excels as one, and she has won the admiration and love of both her peers and the children she works with.

The time had come for Michael, Jessica's fiancé, to come back to the States, and he promptly arrived and was now stationed in Georgia. He communicated with Jessica and asked her to join him. Sergeant Jessica Acosta neatly packed her bags and prepared to venture on to the next chapter of her life. It may not be the chapter she was thinking it was, but it was another chapter nevertheless.

Jessica arrived in Georgia in the spring of '08, a good time for enjoying those luscious Georgian peaches. Jessica was now in Georgia with her fiancé; this chapter of her life was fraught with many a twists and turns and plot changes. She noticed how Michael over the period of his deployment had changed considerably. Changes that challenged Jessica's core system of beliefs. Michael's behavior and system of beliefs had altered quite a bit. Without going into too many details, what happened between them caused Jessica to reevaluate her situation; and the long story short, she decided to pack her bags one more time and leave Georgia and Michael behind.

And so Sergeant Jessica Acosta came back to Portland, Oregon. To a large extent Jessica was heartbroken and devastated and rightfully so.

I had the unique opportunity to meet with her and assuage her distraught feelings. I prayed with her and reminded her that the GOD who knit her in her mother's womb, the GOD who knew all the days of her life even before one of them came to be had also prearranged and predestined everything she will ever need to face this moment in time. And if she allowed, God's SPIRIT would minister to her, and in HIM she will find at a much-deeper level a GOD who cares for all the details of her life and one who has her best interests in mind.

Jessica trusted GOD and went about her life; she found some work at a neighborhood fitness center to help support herself and also to help continue her ministry to the Sunday school children at her local church. The children embraced her (literally) and warmly welcomed her back. Her commitment to her ministry has remained strong ever since.

In the Gospel account of John 5:1-15, there is this story I would like for you to consider:

1 Sometime later, Jesus went up to Jerusalem for a feast of the Jews. 2 Now there is in Jerusalem near the Sheep Gate a pool, which in Aramaic is called Bethesda and which is surrounded by five covered colonnades. 3 Here a great number of disabled people used to lie—the blind, the lame, the paralyzed. 5 One who was there had been an invalid for thirty-eight years. 6 When Jesus saw him lying there and learned that he had been in this condition for a long time, he asked him, "Do you want to get well?"

7 "Sir," the invalid replied, "I have no one to help me into the pool when the water is stirred. While I am trying to get in, someone else goes down ahead of me."

8 Then Jesus said to him, "Get up! Pick up your mat and walk." 9 At once the man was cured; he picked up his mat and walked.

9 The day on which this took place was a Sabbath, 10 and so the Jews said to the man who had been healed, "It is the Sabbath; the law forbids you to carry your mat."

11 But he replied, "The man who made me well said to me, 'Pick up your mat and walk.'"

12 So they asked him, "Who is this fellow who told you to pick it up and walk?"

13 The man who was healed had no idea who it was, for Jesus had slipped away into the crowd that was there.

14 Later Jesus found him at the temple and said to him, "See, you are well again. Stop sinning or something worse may happen to you." 15 The man went away and told the Jews that it was Jesus who had made him well.

Belzatha was the name of the place; some translations refer to it Bethsaida or Bethesda. A temple porch wherein lay this man who had been waiting for thirty-eight years. He had been waiting for his turn for thirty-eight years; he had been waiting for his turn to get into the water (the water is said to have healing powers whenever an angel of the LORD came and stirred it). But no matter how hard he tried, there was always someone who got in ahead of him. There he lay faithfully waiting. His faithfulness, however, was never in question.

JESUS approached the man and asked the man if he wanted to get well. Not knowing who JESUS was, the man reiterated his story. JESUS had compassion on him and healed him right then and there. One of the most wonderful qualities about this man is his patience; he patiently waited even if he had no good results. Year after year, decade after decade, he stayed there unwavering in his hope that one day he would get healed. Anyone I know would have thrown in the towel a lot sooner than that and declared it a lost cause. In the world we live in, we are often surrounded by people who want instant gratification.

But GOD is never that way. HE takes HIS time. HE carefully and methodically orchestrates everything for the good of HIS children. HE does not waver, none whatsoever. You can also see clearly that in this story that the BIBLE says, JESUS found the man, not once but twice. HE looked for HIM and went to HIM. That is what we need to understand as individuals—that GOD will find you, irrespective of circumstances. The hope you have will lead HIM to you.

There are three things to learn from this biblical account of Jesus's healing:

1. The man did not give up.
2. JESUS found the man.
3. The man was healed.

It did not matter what the man's friends or relatives thought about him or his condition. They could have easily said that his biological clock is ticking or ticked away. It didn't matter. He never gave up. I often wonder about the amount of pressure that he must have felt about his life and his situation, from others and from himself. Stress and anxiety and a feeling of hopelessness should have been high on his agenda. In our times people seek chemical dependency for a lot less stress and anxiety. But not this man. His capability to stay focused on the belief that he was going to be healed "come what may" is paramount.

The text doesn't say that JESUS accidentally found the man or by chance ran into him; I believe Jesus's move was very deliberate and calculated. He knew who needed him and when. Our job is simply to trust in his timing because at the end of the day, it would not matter what anybody said or did, as long as you had an encounter with Jesus and you were healed. GOD will find you. He knows what you're going through. He understands your pain; and here's the important part, in his time, he will deliver, in ways that you never thought possible.

There's an old saying that says, "There is no substitute for hard work," and I personally believe that there is no substitute for genuine faith either. Many would like to cruise away on someone else's faith. The Bible says without faith it is impossible to please GOD, and everyone who comes to HIM must believe he exists.

People argue and move toward everything else but a simple trust in their maker because it makes them uncomfortable to say the least. Human wisdom only takes us so far, but for the rest of the way, we must hopelessly rely on faith. Faith and faith alone will draw you closer to your maker. You have to realize that GOD has made it ever so simple and that in order for anyone to go to HIM, all we need is just a simple faith. No ritual, no rite, no routine, no tradition, and certainly not even religion, as the apostle PAUL rightly put it in Romans 1:17: "The Just shall live by faith."

Romans 1:17 says,

17 For in the gospel a righteousness from God is revealed, a righteousness that is by faith from first to last, just as it is written: "The righteous will live by faith."[1]

I believe that is where Jessica is right now in her life. She hasn't given up. Sure the pressures of the modern-day biological clock

---

[1] Romans 1:17 or "is from faith to faith"; Habakkuk 2:4, courtesy of Zondervan and International Bible Society.

is ticking away, but she is staying steadfast. She does not have all the answers (but then again who does). Jessica has recently been admitted to graduate school, and she is pursuing her GOD-given goals, and (as of the writing of this book) she has met someone and is trusting GOD for a wonderful outcome. I personally believe that the wonderful outcome will be all hers. She has a genuine faith and is willing to do what it takes, whatever it takes to see her blessing come through. Whether it be a crippled man by a pool near Bethesda two thousand years ago or whether it be Abraham or Moses or Gideon or David or any of the biblical characters, they all had to wait until it was time for GOD Almighty to work in their lives. Surprisingly, what was true for Abraham is also true for Jessica. The important thing is, not that we all find all the blessings in life but rather that we find the blesser. Search only for the blessing, and you will miss out on the ever-loving arms of our ABBA Father. Once you find his ever-loving arms, he will embrace you; and once in that embrace, you will hear HIS still-small voice echoing in your ears:

> And Lo I will be with you always, even until the end of this age.

Chapter 7

Even Then

I don't know her name or where she grew up or how she lived, but I met her in a store on a sunny July 4 afternoon. She was young, probably in her early twenties; from the looks of it seemed like she had been through some mind-boggling accident. Her one leg was missing from her knee down, and the other leg was mangled like the aftermath of a terrible fire accident. She had a wooden stump on one leg and gently hopped on it. It was a hot summer afternoon, and she was wearing a colorful pair of shorts. Not a care in the world. (I could tell from the way she conducted herself.) She seemed to be a very self-confident person and carried herself as if her beauty flowed from somewhere else. (Her strong self-esteem, I believe!)

Yet on another occasion I met this old man with a severely deformed nose. There it was, right in the middle of his face like a mangled big brown cauliflower. One of my greatest faux pas[2] of all times might as well have been this one occasion when I asked the old man about his nose. I remember my comment went something like this, "It's not even Halloween yet! What have you got there on your nose?" The bad part may have been that I really believed that it was an attachment of some kind; surely, no one would have such a grotesque nose. He calmly looked at me and said something like this, "What's on my nose?"

It just hit me then that the entirety of that overgrown brown cauliflower-looking thing in the center of his face was nothing more than his GOD-given nose. You know he wasn't trying to

---

2   A faux pas (pronounced /ˌfoʊˈpɑː/, plural: faux pas) is a violation of accepted social norms (for example, standard customs or etiquette rules), en.wikipedia.org/wiki/Faux_pas.

cover it up or hide from it. If anything he seemed very calm and incredibly confident about his appearance.

From time to time, I've been immensely encouraged by people whose self-awareness and sense of self-esteem is way above average, and I am excited to have had the privilege and the opportunity to have run into these fine individuals. They have helped me a great deal in my own shortcomings on the way I feel about appearances and impressions I leave on people.

Here is the Bible's description of the personhood of JESUS as found in the book of Isaiah:[3]

Isaiah 53

1 Who has believed our message 1 and to whom has the arm of the Lord been revealed?

2 He grew up before him like a tender shoot, 2 and like a root out of dry ground. 2 He had no beauty

---

[3] Isaiah 53:8 or "from arrest"; "away," Yet who of his generation considered / that he was cut off from the land of the living / for the transgression of my people, / to whom the blow was due?

or majesty to attract us to him, 2 nothing in his appearance that we should desire him.

3 He was despised and rejected by men, 3 a man of sorrows, and familiar with suffering. 3 Like one from whom men hide their faces 3 he was despised, and we esteemed him not.

4 Surely he took up our infirmities 4 and carried our sorrows, 4 yet we considered him stricken by God, 4 smitten by him, and afflicted.

5 But he was pierced for our transgressions, 5 he was crushed for our iniquities; 5 the punishment that brought us peace was upon him, 5 and by his wounds we are healed.

By this description of JESUS, we can clearly understand that he wasn't much to look at. Jesus could have gone for the looks and the wherewithal to fit in with the cool people of his time. But he set an example once and for all. We give so much importance to the outside. John the Baptist, another powerful biblical character, wasn't much to look at either; but when he spoke, people changed their lifestyles. One could argue that in their unique way, they looked extremely beautiful. I would agree, beauty is indeed in the eye of the beholder; but addressing the myriad with self-confidence and self-esteem issues, there's only one thing to say. If anyone could have made himself extremely attractive (by virtue of the definition of external beauty), it was JESUS, but he lived in such a way to show that what really matters is on the inside. If we gained strength from knowing a GOD who strengthens us from within, who watches our every move, who never lets us slip or stumble away, a GOD who never slumbers or sleeps, it is truly a magnificent experience knowing and serving an almighty and an all-powerful GOD.

Down here (on earth) we tend to place way too much importance on the external looks (not all of it is bad), but real self-awareness comes from knowing oneself and that knowing in turn contributes to having an abundant supply of self-confidence. JESUS's example of living and dying was unlike any other in comparison.

Is it possible to not worry? To not care, from what I have seen and what I have read? *Yes*, it is indeed possible.

Early on in life I had my mother as a great encourager, always challenging and motivating me. Her words to me still echoes in my ears, "You can do anything you want. I know you can." She never gave me any kind of a doubt that she didn't believe what she was saying. She always communicated how proud she was of me.

I consider myself to be very blessed to have people around me who trusted me and encouraged me to be my very best. I have run into so many who have had a tougher row to hoe. This can be changed if each and every one of us made just a small contribution to be a positive influence in someone else's life.

When I first became a Christian or a Christ follower, I was touched by one of the greatest verses in the Bible. You could say that it spoke to me at a very deep level. It made me (on the inside of course) run up and down the stairs and do the cha-cha-cha on one hand while standing upside down (if it's hard for you to imagine, simply don't). The verse I am talking about is found at Philippians 4:13:

Philippians 4[4]

13 I can do all *things* through Christ which strengtheneth me.

However, I needed a daily strengthening, a daily assurance, a daily building up—that sort of a help can only be gotten from an ever-present help, our savior JESUS CHRIST.

There may be many who are dissatisfied with themselves, and they spend a fortune on their appearances, only to be unhappy even further with the results, and there are others chasing some other pipe dream that would not satisfy as well.

There is a place to get all of life's meaningful assurances on a regular basis, but it's locked up. The way to open it is to use the key of faith. Faith in what JESUS taught and said comes alive as we step outside the realms of our comfort zone and engage with the all-sufficient savior.

HIS promise that HE will always be there for you builds you from the inside out. Test this out in your own life in small but

---

[4]   KJV, courtesy of Zondervan and International Bible Society.

deliberate ways and watch the power of HIS promises unleash the "I can do anything" person in you. And HE will guide you through all the way for HE has promised,

And Lo I will be with you always, even until the end of this age.

References

1. Ilan, Tal. 2002. *Lexicon of Jewish Names in Late Antiquity Part I: Palestine 330 BCE-200 CE (Texte und Studien zum Antiken Judentum 91)*. Tübingen, Germany: JCB Mohr, 129.

2. Stern, David. 1992. *Jewish New Testament Commentary*. Clarksville, Maryland: Jewish New Testament Publications, 4-5.

3. *The Catholic Encyclopedia*. "Origin of the Name Jesus Christ."

Chapter 8

Let It Go

Bulgaria a country situated at the crossroads of Western Europe, Africa, and Asia. It forms the gateway to three of these continents. If you're completely unfamiliar with this region and its geography and its rich cultural and historical heritage, you can be reminded as I was that Bulgaria was the geographical location where the story of the famous gladiator Spartacus is said to have taken place. Hollywood has made Spartacus sufficiently popular in America and elsewhere, and the history of that story is said to have taken place within the regions of modern-day Bulgaria.

My curiosity into this region wasn't aroused by the legendary Spartacus, but rather by an Olympian by name Nevena Evtimova. She is the kind of person that gets your attention by just saying hello. Her strong Bulgarian accent makes you turn your head and follow the sound and draws you closer to listen to what she has to say, and most times she can give you an ear full.

Nevena was born in communist Bulgaria. Her hopes and dreams of becoming successful in life brought her to the shorelines of America. The hard lessons learned from communist Bulgaria had shaped and molded her into making the best of every opportunity that life threw her way.

Early on in life she was recognized for her athletic abilities in her home country of Bulgaria. God had blessed this lean-framed Eastern European girl with the gift of running, and boy could she run. She ran to the delight of everyone in her nation and never left the victory stands of Bulgaria. Nevena ran the 1,500 meters and the 800 meters and the 4X400 meter relay. Nevena was a solid long-distance runner. She ran with such grace and elegance that won her her victory every single time. Bulgaria however decided to try her skills out in a much-longer and grueling race, the twenty-six-mile marathon. I guess communist Bulgaria wasn't going to take no for an answer. Nevena started her training and began to compete in the marathon. Little did she know that Bulgaria had other plans for Nevena. They saw in her the incredible potential she had and decided to send her to the Summer Olympics. The year was 1984, and the Olympics were to be held in Los Angeles, USA. Nevena came to the shores of America, representing Bulgaria. She ran the best race of her life, and she placed fifteenth in this event. That was a marvelous attempt to take on a grueling twenty-six-mile marathon in the arena of the world's finest athletes. I personally believe that the depth of her accomplishment still eludes her.

God opened doors for her in her newfound country of the U.S. of A. Nevena had immigrated to America to experience and enjoy the luxuries of the democratic process and freedom that it so profusely promises to all its inhabitants. But American freedom came with a price. Nevena now had to start all over again; she needed to put all her best talents and gifts to use in order to make it in capitalist America. That meant new life lessons and new challenges. Once again the long-distance runner geared up to meet the new challenges of life. Nevena knew that things weren't going to be handed to her over a silver platter, but like always she rose up to the challenge, and like a true runner she never looked back. Nevena's unwavering tenacity and youthful stamina helped her go the distance. She became a real estate agent, a car salesperson, and so on and so forth. She excelled in all of these areas. She honed her language (English) skills and consistently and constantly made a steady progress, climbing up the social rungs of life. Her faith and strength of belief in God Almighty was also consistently and constantly growing through the ebb and flow of life.

She began to experience the hand of God meticulously and thoroughly working through her life. God was certainly orchestrating the events of her life, and Nevena never looked back. Nevena is now a forty-three-year-old ex-Olympian living with her aging parents and a teenage daughter. The struggles of life still keep her occupied; she lost her home in the economic downturn the nation had been experiencing. She found it hard to let her hard-earned capital go as she lost her home. She lost the bulk of the real estate business also due to the economic downturn. I met her right around the time when things were beginning to fall apart for her. She was still strong and offered to help anywhere possible in the church's ministry. I talked to her a little bit, and I could feel the stress and pressure of the amount of effort she had put in to hold things together and also how she was giving a thousand percent of whatever she can just so she could save her home. After a lot of discussion, I told her, "Nevena! Just let it go." As much as I didn't want to verbalize those words, I had to because I was convinced beyond a shadow of a doubt that the God who had brought her thus far will see her through the rest of the way. I could see He started a good work in her life and that wasn't about to stop for any reason whatsoever. After our meeting, Nevena sat there somewhat dazed, and I think she was wondering why I said what I said, why I said, "Just let it go." But I could see her burden slowly lifting off. She eased her shoulders, comfortably settled in her chair (previously, she was almost sitting on the edge of her chair), shrugged a little bit, and breathed what looked like a sigh of relief. That day, Nevena, in so many ways, simply "let it go." She stopped fighting her way to keep things from falling apart. The house she cherished so much was foreclosed and sold in an auction. She "let it go." The real estate company she was part of went belly up. She simply "let it go." Her application for employment was turned down in more than a few places, and once again, Nevena simply "let it go." And one after another, things came tumbling down, and Nevena simply "let it all go." She got involved with our church, and she (even in her condition) raised enough money to reroof and repaint the church, and the church got a complete makeover. The money flowed through her. The church was immensely thankful.

The book of Samuel in the Old Testament has a fascinating story, and let me share it with you. It is found from 1 Samuel 1:1 to 1 Samuel 2:11:

1 Samuel 1

1 The Birth of Samuel

1 There was a certain man from Ramathaim, a Zuphite from the hill country of Ephraim, whose name was Elkanah son of Jeroham, the son of Elihu, the son of Tohu, the son of Zuph, an Ephraimite. 2

He had two wives; one was called Hannah and the other Peninnah. Peninnah had children, but Hannah had none.

3 Year after year this man went up from his town to worship and sacrifice to the Lord Almighty at Shiloh, where Hophni and Phinehas, the two sons of Eli, were priests of the Lord. 4 Whenever the day came for Elkanah to sacrifice, he would give portions of the meat to his wife Peninnah and to all her sons and daughters. 5 But to Hannah he gave a double portion because he loved her, and the Lord had closed her womb. 6 And because the Lord had closed her womb, her rival kept provoking her in order to irritate her. 7 This went on year after year. Whenever Hannah went up to the house of the Lord, her rival provoked her till she wept and would not eat. 8 Elkanah her husband would say to her, "Hannah, why are you weeping? Why don't you eat? Why are you downhearted? Don't I mean more to you than ten sons?"

9 Once when they had finished eating and drinking in Shiloh, Hannah stood up. Now Eli the priest was sitting on a chair by the doorpost of the Lord's temple.[5] 10 In bitterness of soul Hannah wept much and prayed to the Lord. 11 And she made a vow, saying, "O Lord Almighty, if you will only look upon your servant's misery and remember me, and not forget your servant but give her a son, then I will give him to the Lord for all the days of his life, and no razor will ever be used on his head."

12 As she kept on praying to the Lord, Eli observed her mouth. 13 Hannah was praying in her heart, and her lips were moving but her voice was not heard. Eli thought she was drunk 14 and said to her, "How long will you keep on getting drunk? Get rid of your wine."

15 "Not so, my lord," Hannah replied, "I am a woman who is deeply troubled. I have not been

---

[5] NIV, 1 Samuel 1:1 to 1 Samuel 2:11.

drinking wine or beer; I was pouring out my soul to the Lord. 16 Do not take your servant for a wicked woman; I have been praying here out of my great anguish and grief."

17 Eli answered, "Go in peace, and may the God of Israel grant you what you have asked of him."

18 She said, "May your servant find favor in your eyes." Then she went her way and ate something, and her face was no longer downcast.

19 Early the next morning they arose and worshiped before the Lord and then went back to their home at Ramah. Elkanah lay with Hannah his wife, and the Lord remembered her. 20 So in the course of time Hannah conceived and gave birth to a son. She named him Samuel saying, "Because I asked the Lord for him."

21 Hannah Dedicates Samuel

21 When the man Elkanah went up with all his family to offer the annual sacrifice to the Lord and to fulfill his vow, 22 Hannah did not go. She said to

her husband, "After the boy is weaned, I will take him and present him before the Lord, and he will live there always."

23 "Do what seems best to you," Elkanah her husband told her. "Stay here until you have weaned him; only may the Lord make good his word." So the woman stayed at home and nursed her son until she had weaned him.

24 After he was weaned, she took the boy with her, young as he was, along with a three-year-old bull an ephah of flour and a skin of wine, and brought him to the house of the Lord at Shiloh. 25 When they had slaughtered the bull, they brought the boy to Eli, 26 and she said to him, "As surely as you live, my lord, I am the woman who stood here beside you praying to the Lord. 27 I prayed for this child, and the Lord has granted me what I asked of him. 28 So now I give him to the Lord. For his whole life he will be given over to the Lord." And he worshiped the Lord there.

1 Samuel 2

1 Hannah's Prayer

1 Then Hannah prayed and said: 1 "My heart rejoices in the Lord; 1 in the Lord my horn is lifted high. 1 My mouth boasts over my enemies, 1 for I delight in your deliverance.

2 "There is no one holy like the Lord; 2 there is no one besides you; 2 there is no Rock like our God.

3 "Do not keep talking so proudly 3 or let your mouth speak such arrogance, 3 for the Lord is a God who knows, 3 and by him deeds are weighed.

4 "The bows of the warriors are broken, 4 but those who stumbled are armed with strength.

5 "Those who were full hire themselves out for food, 5 but those who were hungry hunger no more. 5 She who was barren has borne seven children, 5 but she who has had many sons pines away.

6 "The Lord brings death and makes alive; 6 he brings down to the grave[6] and raises up. 7 The Lord sends poverty and wealth; 7 he humbles and he exalts. 8 He raises the poor from the dust 8 and lifts the needy from the ash heap; 8 he seats them with princes 8 and has them inherit a throne of honor. 8 For the foundations of the earth are the Lord's; 8 upon them he has set the world.

9 "He will guard the feet of his saints, 9 but the wicked will be silenced in darkness. 9 It is not by strength that one prevails; 10 those who oppose the Lord will be shattered. 10 He will thunder against them from heaven; 10 the Lord will judge the ends of the earth. 10 He will give strength to his king 10 and exalt the horn of his anointed."

11 Then Elkanah went home to Ramah, but the boy ministered before the Lord under Eli the priest.

---

[6] Courtesy of Zondervan and International Bible Society.

In this Bible story we can see a story of this woman named Hannah. From the beginning it seems like Hannah had been given the short end of the stick. She remains barren, and then she is ridiculed by Elkanah's (Hanna's husband) other wife. To a casual observer it might seem like Hannah didn't get what she deserved. She seemed like a very good person, a devout wife, a pious Israelite, and a very GOD-fearing individual. In hindsight we know that Hannah would become the mother of Samuel, and Samuel ended up being one of the greatest prophets of the Old Testament.

Imagine, if Hannah was told in the midst of all her problems that she shouldn't worry and that she should simply trust GOD and that GOD was going to bless her immensely beyond her wildest imaginations, Hannah could have done one of two things: either she trusted that "encouragement" and waited patiently or she could have taken an inventory of her life and circumstances and concluded that nothing great was ever going to happen to her. And that no god, Jewish or otherwise, was going to help her out (to the best of her knowledge and understanding that is). Hannah chose to believe in GOD Almighty and stepped outside of what she knew of her life and circumstances. I believe this small step of faith from Hannah's part was instrumental for unleashing the torrent of GOD's blessings. Hannah will be remembered for as long as the Bible is read. Hannah made a choice to have faith in GOD, and that's what it all boils down to a choice. So no matter how terrible the circumstances of your life are, choose to have faith in GOD. You'll have nothing to lose but everything to gain.

I believe this is the route that Nevena Evtimova chose for her life. Experience and reasoning and education kept dragging her one way in one direction, and faith and hope and heart kept dragging her the other way. Nevena chose faith, hope and heart. She didn't blame the church, or anything else. As life got harder, Nevena's faith grew stronger. I wasn't sure about all the details of what God was doing in her life, but I was sure that GOD was coming through for Nevena. I vividly remember this one Sunday morning as I was getting ready to preach. Nevena came and asked me if she could give a short testimony (our church is known for these impromptu testimony times). I said, "By all means go ahead." She got up and, in her own sweet way, told the church how God had blessed her, that she didn't have a job and didn't have any money and didn't know how things were going to turn out, that she had lost her home to bank foreclosure, etc., etc. And then she said, "But," and all ears perked up. She continued, "God helped me find this business opportunity, and through that business opportunity, he helped me make some good money for myself." And then she added, "In the last three months [through this business], I have made sixty-five thousand dollars." She was in tears as she thanked God and vowed to continue to be faithful to Him and encouraged the rest of the church to just remain faithful and that God will bless them, and she added, "All you have to do is simply trust HIM."

I might as well not have preached my three-point sermon that Sunday, and here's why: I noticed that in that particular week, I was beginning to get a few more calls than usual and they all (almost all) had only one underlying question. And in case you were curious as to what they were asking about, they wanted to know what this great business opportunity that Nevena had run into and how exactly did she make her sixty-five thousand dollars in just three months.

The challenges of Nevena's life are by no means over. She continues with many of life's struggles, but thus far God has miraculously intervened in every one of those situations, and her faith has moved up in leaps and bounds. And just this last week, before I could finish this chapter, I recall Nevena saying, "I don't know what it is. Things are going so bad, Pastor James, but I have a strange peace about it." And she always finishes her sentence with a "you know what I want to say to you." I nodded and said yes! (My dear!) I know what it is, only too well.

No matter where you find yourself in life, God can accomplish great things in your life, if you will only let Him. And this is probably what Nevena tried to tell me when she said ever so sweetly, "You know what I want to say! Pastor James."

Two thousand years have come and gone since the birth of Christ, and the challenges of these modern days might be slightly different than challenges of the yesteryears; however, if we choose to have faith even in our present circumstances, I believe that our ever-loving GOD will continue to honor that faith and bend heaven and earth if he has to, in order that you and I be blessed. All you need to remember is that his presence is always with you. Because He has ever so boldly declared,

And Lo I will be with you always, even until the end of this age.

Amen.

References

http://en.wikipedia.org/wiki/Spartacus

1. M. Tullius Cicero,

2. Plutarch, *Crassus* 8

3. Appian, *Civil Wars* 1.116

4. Florus, *Epitome of Roman History* 2.8

5. The Histories, Sallust, Patrick McGushin, Oxford University Press, 1992, ISBN 0-19-872143-9, 112.

6. Balkan history, Thracian tribes, Maedi.

7. Diodorus Siculus, *Historical Library* Book 12

8. Diodorus Siculus, *Historical Library* Book 16

9. Theucidides, *History of the Peloponnesian War* 2.101

10. Tribes, Dynasts and Kingdoms of Northern Greece: History and Numismatics

Chapter 9

What Can I Do

I met him looking for work at a service station. He seemed fairly normal. It seemed like he loved to read and he was always reading something. From what I gathered from him, he seemed to have grown here, there, and everywhere. He was well acquainted with foster-care system of the US government. He was a product of one himself. His name was Preston Mitchell. He seemed somewhat shy of his real name and went with a much cooler-sounding Press. I didn't push the issue any further. I knew with time he would eventually tell me what his original name sounded like. (By the way, he never bothered to volunteer, but I found out anyway!)

His curiosity was bright. He wanted to know more about himself and the world around him. I occasionally caught glimpses into his thought process. And I found him to be fascinated with world events and the issues and concerns that drove humanity in its many different directions. His reading and watching of many documentaries led him often to be perplexed at how misinformed the people were about national and international affairs, and his own personal perception about the world at large was also constantly changing.

One day I saw a rather dejected Press, and so I poked and prodded to find out as to what was happening in his life and if there was anything that I could do to help him. He seemed rather reluctant at first, but then a little later, he just made a comment like, "This world is just a bad place." I knew enough not to say much right away and simply allowed him to brew on that topic for a while. Then he slowly started with an "Ahem," and I followed it closely with a "What are you going to do about it?" The answer he gave is the reason for my writing this chapter.

He replied as sincerely as a twenty-two-year-old could: "What can I do?" And as if that didn't sound hopeless and dejected enough, he followed it with an even more depressing "I don't know what to do!" Such is the human predicament; oftentimes, we perceive what the problems are (to varying degrees of course), and there arises a deep longing and groaning if you will to get up and do something about it. But what? The question of humanity to most of its perceived problems is simply "What can I do" or "I don't know what to do."

Several Bible characters have gone through somewhat of a similar feeling of despair. I am specifically reminded of this one Old Testament story. The story is found in the book of Daniel 3. The story goes like this:

Daniel 3:1-30[7]

1 The Image of Gold and the Fiery Furnace

1 King Nebuchadnezzar made an image of gold, ninety feet high and nine feet wide, and set it up

---

[7] NIV, courtesy of Zondervan and International Bible Society.

on the plain of Dura in the province of Babylon. 2 He then summoned the satraps, prefects, governors, advisers, treasurers, judges, magistrates and all the other provincial officials to come to the dedication of the image he had set up. 3 So the satraps, prefects, governors, advisers, treasurers, judges, magistrates and all the other provincial officials assembled for the dedication of the image that King Nebuchadnezzar had set up, and they stood before it.

4 Then the herald loudly proclaimed, "This is what you are commanded to do, O peoples, nations and men of every language: 5 As soon as you hear the sound of the horn, flute, zither, lyre, harp, pipes and all kinds of music, you must fall down and worship the image of gold that King Nebuchadnezzar has set up. 6 Whoever does not fall down and worship will immediately be thrown into a blazing furnace."

7 Therefore, as soon as they heard the sound of the horn, flute, zither, lyre, harp and all kinds of music, all the peoples, nations and men of every language

fell down and worshiped the image of gold that King Nebuchadnezzar had set up.

8 At this time some astrologers came forward and denounced the Jews. 9 They said to King Nebuchadnezzar, "O king, live forever! 10 You have issued a decree, O king, that everyone who hears the sound of the horn, flute, zither, lyre, harp, pipes and all kinds of music must fall down and worship the image of gold, 11 and that whoever does not fall down and worship will be thrown into a blazing furnace. 12 But there are some Jews whom you have set over the affairs of the province of Babylon—Shadrach, Meshach and Abednego—who pay no attention to you, O king. They neither serve your gods nor worship the image of gold you have set up."

13 Furious with rage, Nebuchadnezzar summoned Shadrach, Meshach and Abednego. So these men were brought before the king, 14 and Nebuchadnezzar said to them, "Is it true, Shadrach, Meshach and Abednego, that you do not serve my gods or worship the image of

gold I have set up? 15 Now when you hear the sound of the horn, flute, zither, lyre, harp, pipes and all kinds of music, if you are ready to fall down and worship the image I made, very good. But if you do not worship it, you will be thrown immediately into a blazing furnace. Then what god will be able to rescue you from my hand?"

16 Shadrach, Meshach and Abednego replied to the king, "O Nebuchadnezzar, we do not need to defend ourselves before you in this matter. 17 If we are thrown into the blazing furnace, the God we serve is able to save us from it, and he will rescue us from your hand, O king. 18 But even if he does not, we want you to know, O king, that we will not serve your gods or worship the image of gold you have set up."

19 Then Nebuchadnezzar was furious with Shadrach, Meshach and Abednego, and his attitude toward them changed. He ordered the furnace heated seven times hotter than usual 20 and commanded some of the strongest soldiers in his army to tie up

Shadrach, Meshach and Abednego and throw them into the blazing furnace. 21 So these men, wearing their robes, trousers, turbans and other clothes, were bound and thrown into the blazing furnace. 22 The king's command was so urgent and the furnace so hot that the flames of the fire killed the soldiers who took up Shadrach, Meshach and Abednego, 23 and these three men, firmly tied, fell into the blazing furnace.

24 Then King Nebuchadnezzar leaped to his feet in amazement and asked his advisers, "Weren't there three men that we tied up and threw into the fire?"

24 They replied, "Certainly, O king."

25 He said, "Look! I see four men walking around in the fire, unbound and unharmed, and the fourth looks like a son of the gods."

26 Nebuchadnezzar then approached the opening of the blazing furnace and shouted, "Shadrach, Meshach and Abednego, servants of the Most High God, come out! Come here!"

26 So Shadrach, Meshach and Abednego came out of the fire, 27 and the satraps, prefects, governors and royal advisers crowded around them. They saw that the fire had not harmed their bodies, nor was a hair of their heads singed; their robes were not scorched, and there was no smell of fire on them.

28 Then Nebuchadnezzar said, "Praise be to the God of Shadrach, Meshach and Abednego, who has sent his angel and rescued his servants! They trusted in him and defied the king's command and were willing to give up their lives rather than serve or worship any god except their own God. 29 Therefore I decree that the people of any nation or language who say anything against the God of Shadrach, Meshach and Abednego be cut into pieces and their houses be turned into piles of rubble, for no other god can save in this way."

30 Then the king promoted Shadrach, Meshach and Abednego in the province of Babylon.

King Nebuchadnezzar, a Persian king, issues a decree that everyone in his kingdom should bow before this ninety-foot statue that he had erected; and I believe, it was a statue of himself. And what else, the king adds that if someone doesn't bow down to this statue then they will be thrown into a blazing furnace (verse 11).

Needless to say that there were these three God-fearing men by names Shadrach, Meshach, and Abednego who did not want to comply with this new government regulation. They had understood it clearly that the God they worshiped made it clear that under no circumstances they are to worship an idol.

Word got around in that town that somehow these three men weren't following the new government regulations, and the villains of the story soon let the king's officers know what was going on in their neighborhood. So the king summoned the three God-fearing men to come and see him. And the story continues that they went to see him, and lo and behold, the king was completely upset with their behavior. Nevertheless, he gave them a second chance. He said (and I paraphrase), "I'll give you, guys, another chance, and this time, as soon as you hear the musical instruments playing, I want you to bow down before this statue and worship it."

Much like Press, Shadrach, Meshach, and Abednego knew things weren't right; and much like Press's answer, they didn't know what to do. Or more importantly, what can they do? But one thing was for certain, they did not comply with that new law. Now the time had come for them to face the consequences of their actions.

Even in their ignorance of not knowing what to do, Shadrach, Meshach, and Abednego did three things:

1. They identified that what was being asked of everyone including them was not okay. That's often the first step: identify what is wrong as clearly as possible.

2. They didn't go along with that which was wrong even though the consequences were severe. There must have been this one day or this one moment in time when Shadrach, Meshach, and Abednego either individually or collectively made up their minds that enough was enough. Sure they may have to pay for it with their lives. But they

decided to stand up for what they believe in. A moment like that is a life-altering moment, a moment like that is when you leave the pack behind, a moment like that is a what I call a breakthrough moment, a moment like that puts you squarely in the answer circle. You are no longer part of the wondering crowd or the wandering crowd. You are now part of a solution. No one guarantees you any success or medals or crowns (of this world anyway), but you see you didn't do it for those reasons. Will you be fearful during this process? Heck yeah! (Sorry, there's no nice way to communicate that emotion.) Would it shake the foundations of all your goals and your aspirations? Once again, a nice, solid heck yeah! Shadrach, Meshach, and Abednego had to face the king on account of their decision making. They were indeed the radicals of their time, and as such, they took their place in history. They made history with the decisions they had to make.

3. They demonstrated that having faith must be accompanied by works. You have to back it up with some actions. They could have said, "We have faith, but we know GOD will

understand why we had to worship the idol. We were forced, and as such, it's not our fault. Surely, a loving GOD doesn't want us to be thrown into a furnace." While that reasoning doesn't sound so unreasonable, had they followed through with that reasoning, they would have missed an encounter with the Almighty.

The king was now left with the difficult decision of having to punish Shadrach, Meshach, and Abednego. He had to because Shadrach, Meshach, and Abednego had defied his orders; so the king was furious, and he commands the soldiers to turn up the heat in the furnace. He said, "Turn it up seven times hotter than usual." And the soldiers did so. Then the king commanded that the three be tied up and thrown into the furnace. The furnace was so hot that even the soldiers who threw them into the furnace got killed by the heat.

Then something miraculous happened; the king found them walking about in the furnace, yes! That's right—walking about, inside the furnace. Walking and talking with the LORD.

I wonder what their conversation must have been like. When they came out, there was no second-degree burn or third-degree burn. As a matter of fact, there was not even the smell of fire upon them.

You will find several levels of complications come across your path in life, and in each one of those paths, you will be given the opportunity to do something about it or to simply stand along the shorelines, and wonder as to what could have been or should have been.

Don't lose your place in history by being complacent; don't lose the opportunity to make a difference (no matter how small). Press may never have figured it out; but you, my dear friend, are GOD's instrument. What you say and do is going to set a series of possibilities into motion for you and everyone else. I wonder what great accomplishments of human history are awaiting your response. Today is your day, and this moment is your moment. By all means, seize the day and the moment.

More important than my words and thoughts and encouragements if any that I can offer you through this book is the overwhelming comfort that there is someone who is going to stand by you, someone who couldn't wait for you to start living a faith-driven life, someone who longs to bless your life. That someone is our savior and Christ the LORD JESUS himself. And he is going to be with you every step of the way. And this is his promise to you:

And Lo I will be with you always, even until the end of this age.

Chapter 10

Radio

I was invited by my friend to fill in for her radio show in Portland, Oregon. I haven't been on a radio show before, so I ventured into the station, ahead of schedule, and there was just one guy there. He let me in after I told him I was sitting in for my friend. (And he assumed I knew what I was doing.) He seemed to be in control in that he was perfectly able to handle the affairs of this radio station all by himself (at least for the time being).

I was shown into this soundproof room, and there in that room was nothing or nobody. Somehow, I was supposed to be on air from there on for the next forty-five minutes. I had to keep talking (mostly to myself, and guess what, writing became the next logical step, right!) into the microphone. This wasn't one of those call-in radio shows although it should have been.

So there I was talking to myself, and the one guy who was there—I found out later—was the sound engineer. He was busy doing his own thing, and all he said was "When the time is up, you'll see me over there. I'll show you five fingers, and you've got five minutes to wind it all up." He eventually had to give me a three-minute warning and a one-minute warning, and then it was all over.

I had so much fun—talking to myself, that is. I had an excellent feedback from the church congregation. Hope I didn't fail to mention that I had mentioned the airing of this show and its timing to a few people at church (okay! a lot of people, I am sorry).

The verdict was this: "It was just like one of your sermons at church." Hopefully, I am not always talking to myself at church. I took that as a compliment. (Wait a minute! Did they mean the sermon was equally boring? I don't think so!?)

I am an optimist, so I imagined them lovingly say that it was great. But imagine if JESUS had a call-in radio show. (It's not blasphemous! So calm down.)

First of all, it would be the hottest show on earth.

Second of all, even though the number of callers would be immensely high, somehow the lines would never be too busy for anybody. Princes and paupers would both get the same treatment.

How about that?

Third of all, it would be a multilingual show. Anybody from anywhere can call in, speak in their own language (there will no special signage with a se habla español needed!), and expect to be perfectly understood. (You don't have to keep repeating yourself and getting louder for no good reason.) There will be no "You know what I mean" at the end of every sentence because he'll completely understand what you mean even before you could verbalize the question.

And last of all, it will be personal. You can't call in and go "Ahem, this is . . . Tommy . . . uh . . . um . . . Jones." And JESUS would be "Hey, David, how's it going?" You can be rest assured that he is talking to you, the caller, every caller. Simultaneously, and if he chooses, he can make it a private conversation just between you and HIM.

This is entirely possible, and you know what, you don't even need a radio or a telephone line or anything. The only thing you need to have is faith. Call on HIM with faith today and see what marvelous things he can show you or accomplish through you (Jeremiah 33:1-3).

[1]While Jeremiah was still confined in the courtyard of the guard, the word of the Lord came to him a second time: [2] "This is what the Lord says, he who made the earth, the Lord who formed it and established it—the Lord is his name: [3] 'Call to me and I will answer you and tell you great and unsearchable things you do not know.'"[4]

If you begin to question yourself whether you can talk to HIM today, sitting down in the corner of a room, having too many problems to cope with, stressed out and getting ready for an anxiety attack, wondering if HE will be real to you, questioning if HE will still hear you in spite of everything you've done. Let me tell you something: HE not only hears you, but also cares for you, so much that HE never will leave you or forsake you. I hope you can tune your ears today and hear HIM whisper to you:

And Lo I will be with you always, even until the end of this age.

Chapter 11

Gypsy

In tropical India there lives this tribe of indigenous people called the gypsies. I have watched them hunt and forage with such rudimentary weapons, and they are so incredibly gifted at it. The gypsies, when they hunt, make a certain type of sound; and based on the type of sound they make, they could attract a certain type of animal or bird, which they eventually end up hunting. Modern-day hunters, let's say duck or goose hunters, sometimes use a short reed in order to help them reproduce a certain type of sound that a duck or goose may recognize. But the gypsies simply use the tone of their natural voice and bring in all kinds of birds into their hunting area. I have witnessed them calling in for crows, and I've seen the crow turn in midflight and swoop in straight to the hunter.

The uniqueness of their voice elicits a certain response. GOD's voice is also heard by those who know HIM. He doesn't make a generic sound, but rather he calls us by names Maria, Veena, Anjali, David, Bradley, Gerd, Paula, Angie, Debbie, Kayode, Ona, Wilbis, Dorothy, Jodi, Flo, Kevin, and so on and so forth. And just like a radio needs to be tuned to a certain frequency, so also we need to tune our ears to our master's voice. What one hears makes a critical difference in how one acts and behaves, no matter what the information. If you've gone to a theater and watched a movie, you'll know what I am talking about. Mute the sound effects of the movie, and the movie ceases to be not as moving or as captivating anymore. The sound makes such a critical difference in the response that is elicited.

God's voice is sometimes audible, sometimes still and small and sometimes thundering. In whatever way he chooses to speak with you, all you need to do is to simply respond to HIS voice, to the best of your GOD-given ability. And the success of your life isn't based on your capability to hear HIS voice, but rather it's based on how you choose to respond to what you've heard. Remember, Judas had heard just as much as the other apostles, all firsthand information; yet he chose to go the way of perdition. Something to consider!

As you get older, your experience helps you to see life differently, and that experience also further helps you to contour your life along safe and secure corridors. Imagine if you somehow were able to hear all of your life-altering information upfront. Had I known what I know today, for example, that I would be married to this great girl and have two lovely children and that I would be living in a lovely neighborhood overlooking the mountains and valleys at age forty-three. Even if I didn't know all the details of this life ahead of time, even if I were just told the end result, that would have been great. I wouldn't have worried nearly as much as I did during my lifetime. I worried a lot about where the road of life was leading me and so on and so forth. As human beings we all have the inherent need for certainty. Letting me know that things are going to be taken care of by someone who loves me and cares for me and who has the wherewithal to follow through on all their promises makes living life with passion so much more possible.

That kind of security and certainty is what CHRIST our SAVIOR is offering to anyone who comes to HIM with faith. And that is the only requirement. JESUS said in John 10:10: "The thief cometh not, but for to steal, and to kill, and to destroy: I am come that they might have life, and that they might have it more abundantly."[8]

You can have this abundant life as you step toward HIM in faith. Maybe you're out there and you're thinking I do have faith, then why am I not enjoying this abundant life. You see abundant life isn't a destination but a journey. Don't keep asking the question, "are we there yet?" and miss out on the journey. Life's pitfalls and worries and concerns are no longer yours. You must live with the frame of mind that says, "If I live, I live for Christ. *If* I die, I die for Christ." Believe that in your heart and go out there and live life with passion. This is your day; live it

---

[8]   KJV, courtesy of Zondervan and International Bible Society.

as if it's all you've got. Whatever else tomorrow will bring, let go and let GOD. Can you do it? With faith you can.

I am forty-three now, and if I had heard all the right information while growing up, the only perceivable difference (and this may be arguable based on your world view) to me would be this: I would have chosen the exact same path. But as I said earlier, I would have worried a lot less.

Over the years from the reading of the BIBLE, I am constantly assured by GOD that my life is in his hands; and I personally would have it nowhere else but in his hands because I know, come what may, my life is in HIS hands. And the only thing I would strive toward these days is to learn to live each day without any worries and to live one day at a time. Needless to say, this motivates me to live my life with passion. This in turn exponentially increases the driving force to be a giving person and a contributing person as well.

Life isn't lived in years at a time or decades at a time, but rather a day at a time. One day you're here, and poof, you may be gone the next. GOD, in his omniscience, spoke these words, knowing full well that we will need HIS assurance on a daily

basis; and here it is:

And Lo I will be with you always, even until the

end of this age.

Chapter 12

George William

His name is George William or, as we fondly called him, Brother Bill. The man had a prophetic calling in his life—not so much as foretelling as in predicting the future but in forthtelling as in making proclamations (of the goodness of GOD) or the events as they unfold in the time space continuum.

He was and is what I call an amicable spirit. He got along well with just about everyone. He never seemed to have offended anyone in the course of his lifetime. (I may be exaggerating it, just a bit.) He knew GOD as loving and caring and not as condemning whatsoever. He expounds on the scriptures as a way of life. I believe he would do well with a pulpit and some audience. But he seems equally comfortable with his forthtelling in any geographical location he finds himself in. He makes a living driving the public transportation for the county, and he is very good at what he does almost to a military precision.

He was offered the opportunity to pastor a church in Oklahoma, but he turned it down. From what I understood, I am not sure whether he was following the will of GOD or his own. Either way, that decision-making process still remains fresh in his memories.

Brother Bill, among other things, was a devoutly married man. You would look at him and think (as his coworkers often did) that he seemed like the kind of guy who had it all together. He had a great relationship with his maker and also had a great loving relationship with his spouse. He and his wife worked together for the same organization (public transportation drivers). They both made a decent living, and life was good.

This is what one would have described as a happily-ever-after situation. And it was for twenty-eight years. That's right; his marriage lasted for twenty-eight years. Slowly but surely, GOD revealed to him that his relationship with his wife would suddenly be taking a turn for the worst. So one day, Brother Bill (inspired by the Holy Spirit) confronted his wife; he asked her if things were alright between the two of them or if he should be aware of something that may be happening between her and someone else.

The long story short, she confessed in so many words that she had been seeing someone or at least that there was someone involved in her life and that she was making plans to move on. Bill was devastated; his focus in life, his ambitions, his goals were all suddenly out of whack. He stumbled and stuttered. And he told her, "I thought we were doing well," "I thought you knew JESUS," whatever the case may be, whatever the reasons may be. She had made up her mind to move on, and with time, she followed through with those plans and moved on.

Bill was devastated, confused, bewildered, puzzled, perplexed, baffled, and at a complete loss. He was beginning to wonder "what just happened here? What just happened to my life?"

Brother Bill had somehow lost himself in this process, or as he called it, he had lost his 'mojo'.

I met Brother Bill at a convenience store, and we struck up a conversation. He insisted that we meet one-on-one and somehow allow him the chance to talk about his lot in life. In the beginning I was reluctant to play counselor, but he was Brother Bill, and so I couldn't say no to a brother. However, I told him that I would meet with him as time and opportunity presented itself.

The fact of the matter is I didn't have anything to say to him—I prayed and felt like, if anything, I should just listen to what he had to say. So just like any sane man under the circumstances would do, I postponed the meeting to as far away as I possibly could. But GOD had a unique way of making things happen.

One day, not too long after I promised to meet with him, I (accidentally?) met him in a hardware store of all the places. Standing next to some serious power tools, there we were talking, two grown men discussing about the frailties of life. I decided to continue this discussion ever a cup of coffee or some such.

So we drove off to the nearest fast-food restaurant and ordered a high-calorie value meal (large fries and a quarter pounder) and sat down to wolf it down. And yes, it was anyone's guess; Brother Bill still remained a devastated man who simply wanted to get together and talk, and so we did.

We talked and talked and talked (mostly him), and all I needed to do was just listen. And I listened to this brokenhearted man of GOD. He poured out his life, and he seemed to be very deeply and sincerely hurt (who wouldn't be). His wife of twenty-eight years had left him for someone else. How do you deal with that? Somehow, I am never going to forget it (because he mentioned it often enough). His love for his wife was very sincere. They did everything together, they went on mission trips, and they ministered in various churches and even established new ministry movements. Somehow, things were moving right along, and then this happened out of nowhere.

He seemed like a train wreck; parts of it seemed to make perfect sense, and parts of it didn't make any sense whatsoever. It looked like as if the rails had somehow loosened in several places, and the train seemed like it just wanted to keep forging ahead. The views, the bird's-eye view or whatever, no matter where you observed this train wreck from, it didn't look like much of anything was salvageable.

I didn't tell him that (of course), but I did tell him that the state of affairs was not going to change for him (until GOD intervenes, and that was my only prayer). The wreck had happened. Whatever caused it, whatever happened knowingly or unknowingly, whoever's fault it was—the point is what do we do now? His wife of twenty-eight years was or is deeply hardwired into his circuitry and rightfully so. Needless to say, he was left in shambles. Some aspects of his wife's actions made sense, and most of them just didn't add up.

Bill is a very zealous man for GOD, and his lifestyle included one of prophetic utterances, interpretation of dreams, receiving words of encouragement (in the SPIRIT), exhortation, etc. You see Brother Bill wasn't a Sunday Christian; there was no Off button to his Christianity. His intimate moments with his wife and the rest of his life seemed sporadically laced with long stretches of a prophet's work (exhorting, forethtelling, and praising GOD).

While this was the makeup of Brother Bill, it wasn't (at least from what I understood) who his wife was—and it seemed to me that she had somehow hung in there for twenty eight long years.

As time went by, she must have decided to call it quits and move on. I understand where she comes from (although I may not agree with the modality of her approach). Brother Bill strikes me as an individual who is ready to proclaim GOD's word at a moment's notice (that's a wonderful quality). And the spirit that fuels that engine is an unquenchable spirit, and as such, his life and ministry is of immense consequence. I believe this, above all, prevented him from being just a Sunday Christian, and it may have also landed him in his current predicament.

I wanted to understand more about this paradox. (You want to be a Christian at all the times, and at the same time, you don't want to lose your wife or any of the immediate family and friends.)

If you notice the life and story of any of the Old Testament prophets—whether it be Daniel, Ezekiel, or Jeremiah—the pattern you'll notice in the lives of each of these individuals is that they were all trailblazers of their times. They were never men who went with the flow. If anything they went against the flow, they were often perceived as out of their mind or wild or crazy.

They inevitably were led by GOD, and what they said and did still remains pertinent to our lives. Their sacrifices yielded them names such as weird, crazy, etc.; but they irrevocably remained an anachronism of their era. But what they said and did about 1,500 (or so) years ago still stands the test of time—in terms of its relevance, in terms of its purpose, in terms of its application, in terms of its importance, in terms of its bearing, in terms of its rationale, in terms of its justification, in terms of its validation, in terms of its reason, and in terms of all these and then some. It isn't because of who they were but because who the LORD GOD Almighty, the maker of heaven and earth, is.

I began to see Brother Bill under this lens, and it occurred to me that he fit the mold. He was always filled with zeal and with lots of enthusiasm for who GOD is and what he had done in people's lives.

Brother Bill was a very godly man, if anything he wasn't much of anything else, from what I saw. (But does anyone need to be anything else?) I could see in him all the traits of an Old Testament prophet; he was less belligerent and confrontational than some of them. So, after having some understanding about his calling and his way of life, I told Brother Bill that this is what I perceived of his lifestyle and this is how it is going to be—his prophetic hardwiring isn't going to change, like a common cold or a flu. His convictions were deep, and his need to speak forth GOD's words was even deeper.

So what does all this mean for Brother Bill? Deep in the recesses of Exodus, right around the thirty-fifth chapter, I found something that helped me better understand this predicament.

In this chapter GOD begins to give the Israelites an outline of how the tabernacle should look and function, and the same motif can be seen carried on, all the way to fortieth chapter.

Here is an example of the guidelines that struck me. It is found in Exodus 36:8-38:

> All the skilled men among the workmen made the
> tabernacle with ten curtains of finely twisted linen and

blue, purple and scarlet yarn, with cherubim worked into them by a skilled craftsman. ⁹ All the curtains were the same size—twenty-eight cubits long and four cubits wide.[a] ¹⁰ They joined five of the curtains together and did the same with the other five. ¹¹ Then they made loops of blue material along the edge of the end curtain in one set, and the same was done with the end curtain in the other set. ¹² They also made fifty loops on one curtain and fifty loops on the end curtain of the other set, with the loops opposite each other. ¹³ Then they made fifty gold clasps and used them to fasten the two sets of curtains together so that the tabernacle was a unit.

¹⁴ They made curtains of goat hair for the tent over the tabernacle—eleven altogether. ¹⁵ All eleven curtains were the same size—thirty cubits long and four cubits wide.[b] ¹⁶ They joined five of the curtains into one set and the other six into another set. ¹⁷ Then they made fifty loops along the edge of the end curtain in one set and also along the edge of the end curtain in the

other set. [18] They made fifty bronze clasps to fasten the tent together as a unit. [19] Then they made for the tent a covering of ram skins dyed red, and over that a covering of hides of sea cows.[c]

[20] They made upright frames of acacia wood for the tabernacle. [21] Each frame was ten cubits long and a cubit and a half wide,[d] [22] with two projections set parallel to each other. They made all the frames of the tabernacle in this way. [23] They made twenty frames for the south side of the tabernacle [24] and made forty silver bases to go under them—two bases for each frame, one under each projection. [25] For the other side, the north side of the tabernacle, they made twenty frames [26] and forty silver bases—two under each frame. [27] They made six frames for the far end, that is, the west end of the tabernacle, [28] and two frames were made for the corners of the tabernacle at the far end. [29] At these two corners the frames were double from the bottom all the way to the top and fitted into a single ring;

both were made alike. *30* So there were eight frames and sixteen silver bases—two under each frame.

31 They also made crossbars of acacia wood: five for the frames on one side of the tabernacle, *32* five for those on the other side, and five for the frames on the west, at the far end of the tabernacle. *33* They made the center crossbar so that it extended from end to end at the middle of the frames. *34* They overlaid the frames with gold and made gold rings to hold the crossbars. They also overlaid the crossbars with gold.

35 They made the curtain of blue, purple and scarlet yarn and finely twisted linen, with cherubim worked into it by a skilled craftsman. *36* They made four posts of acacia wood for it and overlaid them with gold. They made gold hooks for them and cast their four silver bases. *37* For the entrance to the tent they made a curtain of blue, purple and scarlet yarn and finely twisted linen—the work of an embroiderer; *38* and they made five posts with hooks for them. They overlaid the tops of the posts and their bands with gold and made their five bases of bronze.

And the rest of the chapters in this book look just like that! The sheer volume of details found in these chapters, the intricate details of all the clothing that Aaron wore down to the type of fire—the chapters here are filled with details and more details; and GOD wanted none of them compromised. No, not even a little. They were to follow everything, down to the details; the punishment for not obeying was often death. Yes, capital punishment. Can you believe it—capital punishment over the details? I have never seen any building project in the world except here, wherein if you didn't follow the details, you could be struck dead. That only goes to show that JEHOVAH (YHWH) GOD was a GOD of details.

He cared about every aspect of the temple, and we know from the New Testament that GOD's SPIRIT no longer resides in the handmade temples anymore, but he resides in the human heart.

1 Corinthians 6

[19] Do you not know that your body is a temple of the Holy Spirit, who is in you, whom you have received from God? You are not your own; [20] you were bought at a price. Therefore honor God with your body.

The Bible declares he is the same yesterday, today, and forever:

Hebrews 13

[8] Jesus Christ is the same yesterday and today and forever.

If that is so (and it is), then the GOD who cared so much about the details of the handmade temple during the Mosaic era is the same GOD who cares about the human temple today.

Once your heart becomes HIS home, then you have the Almighty involved in the details of your life. Now, more than ever, you need to realize that the life you live is no longer yours but HIS. So much so that all you need to do is to sit back, stop worrying, and relax and trust HIM to lead you all the way.

Brother Bill asked me one more question, "Does this mean I goofed up in my relationship? What about those times when I did goof up?" His real question should have been "Can my life be restored again? Can this train wreck be fixed? Can this vessel once again become a vessel of glory? Is it too late? Am I a lost cause? Am I too far gone?"

At first I gave him a (what I considered to be a penetrating) glance and then rephrased his question to him. What he said is important for all of us to hear, and he said and I quote, "I've known the answer all along. I just needed to hear it." I thought about that for a long time. We all need to hear affirmations, from time to time. It doesn't matter how much you know because these affirmations become the building blocks that build you from the inside out. It seems like the distance from the ear to the heart is shorter than the distance from the brain to the heart.

So I gave him a lot of affirmations of who he is and who GOD has made him to be and as to how our GOD cares about all the details of his life and mine and yours. GOD will leave no stone unturned in order that you find HIS favor.

Now consider your life whatever is going on. Yes, that's right. Whatever the issues may be, you are never beyond HIS redemptive reach. Everything I told Brother Bill are things he had already heard and understood. But every affirmation that I can speak out seemed to guide him. I could see the sparkle in his eyes again. And he said and I (once again) quote, "I can slowly feel like I am getting my 'mojo' back."

He wanted to continue to meet from time to time on a one-on-one basis. But my thoughts to the reader is this: GOD cares about the details of your life. By that, I mean all the details of your life testified by witnesses such as Abraham, Moses, Elijah, and Enoch that HE rightly provides for that which you need most at the right time.

Brother Bill needed an encourager, someone who would see his point of view. GOD allowed me in his omniscience to be there for Dean along his journey of life. I have been at the receiving end of such benefits many a time.

The challenge is to have the faith that GOD is the one who can do this, and placing your trust in HIM is never a vain pursuit. And to trust HIM with all the details of your life is the vital ingredient of that trust. No matter where you find yourself in life, you can rest soundly in HIS one true promise:

And Lo I will be with you always, even until the end of this age.

Philippians 4:8, American Standard Version

Finally, brethren, whatsoever things are true, whatsoever things are honorable, whatsoever things are just, whatsoever things are pure, whatsoever things are lovely, whatsoever things are of good report; if there be any virtue, and if there be any praise, think on these things.

Chapter 13

Parenting

Parenting is one of the oldest responsibilities known to mankind. It seems like it's been deeply wired into our systems. I have two daughters, and as such, I have had the privilege of being a parent and watching firsthand how children react and how they grow. Parents seem to pay an awful lot of attention to children at the early developmental stages, and this attention seems to slowly subside with time and occasion.

This is healthy, as long as it is a gradual process; this in turn gives the young adult time and opportunity to break through barriers—cultural, social, or otherwise—and learn the process of decision making and eventually move on to adulthood.

This is a gradual process. For example, let's consider the correlation between infants and baby food. We all know that baby food is the best for infants (until such time you've tasted it yourself, then it's a whole different story). The same, however, doesn't make a proper meal for a growing child. As they show signs of growth, we feed them more and more solid foods if you will. However, we don't feed them a thirty-two-ounce steak right away, but rather we slowly and steadily change their eating habits and sometimes against their will! As a result of this good nutrition, they grow in leaps and bounds at a rather remarkable pace. They may not have quite clearly understood all the ramifications of eating a balanced nutrition and the need for protein and vitamins and minerals, but their system responds amazingly to this nutrition, and you can see them growing in accordance with their age.

Certainly, they are bound to have a few varieties of food that their system would not be able to tolerate. They may throw up one kind of food, they may choke on another, and they may get sick over others, leaving them with a trip to the hospital, a headache, an allergic reaction, and so on and so forth. The adventures of parenthood never end.

Parents somehow seem to have a reasonable grasp about this process. They know that their children will live through this growing-up period and may even master the art of proper eating habits. Parents may be involved in teaching their children the tenets of a proper eating habit, but I've yet to meet a single parent (and I hope I never do!) who is completely consumed with the pressure and the anxiety and the stress over the issue of whether or not their kids will ever have healthy eating habits. I am sure there are going to be some children who don't quite get it when they are really young, but over the course of their lives, they are bound to pick up new information; and as they learn to process that information slowly but surely, they will eventually change and do what is right for their bodies.

I am proposing to you, parents, out there that the level of your worries (about your children's eating habits) isn't directly proportional to the results that produce a healthy eating habit in a growing child's life.

Much like you never really stress out about the eating habits of children, which if any eventually corrects itself, so also in the matter of raising children, the parents are much better-off not worrying or stressing out as much. Certainly, they have the parental responsibility to instill sound moral values in their children; but for goodness sake, there's no medal in heaven or on earth given out to those who worried or got stressed out the most.

Allow me to draw your attention to this Bible story. It is found in Luke 15:11-33:

Luke 15

[11] The Parable of the Lost Son

[11] Jesus continued: "There was a man who had two sons. [12] The younger one said to his father, 'Father, give me my share of the estate.' So he divided his property between them.

[13] "Not long after that, the younger son got together all he had, set off for a distant country and there squandered his wealth in wild living. [14] After he

had spent everything, there was a severe famine in that whole country, and he began to be in need. [15] So he went and hired himself out to a citizen of that country, who sent him to his fields to feed pigs. [16] He longed to fill his stomach with the pods that the pigs were eating, but no one gave him anything.

[17] "When he came to his senses, he said, 'How many of my father's hired men have food to spare, and here I am starving to death! [18] I will set out and go back to my father and say to him: Father, I have sinned against heaven and against you. [19] I am no longer worthy to be called your son; make me like one of your hired men.' [20] So he got up and went to his father.

[20] "But while he was still a long way off, his father saw him and was filled with compassion for him; he ran to his son, threw his arms around him and kissed him.

[21] "The son said to him, 'Father, I have sinned against heaven and against you. I am no longer worthy to be called your son.[a]'

[22] "But the father said to his servants, 'Quick! Bring the best robe and put it on him. Put a ring on his finger and sandals on his feet. [23] Bring the fattened calf and kill it. Let's have a feast and celebrate. [24] For this son of mine was dead and is alive again; he was lost and is found.' So they began to celebrate.

[25] "Meanwhile, the older son was in the field. When he came near the house, he heard music and dancing. [26] So he called one of the servants and asked him what was going on. [27] 'Your brother has come,' he replied, 'and your father has killed the fattened calf because he has him back safe and sound.'

[28] "The older brother became angry and refused to go in. So his father went out and pleaded with him. [29] But he answered his father, 'Look! All these years I've been slaving for you and never disobeyed your orders. Yet you never gave me even a young goat so I could celebrate with my friends. [30] But when this son of yours who has squandered your property with prostitutes comes home, you kill the fattened calf for him!'

[31] "'My son,' the father said, 'you are always with me, and everything I have is yours. [32] But we had to celebrate and be glad, because this brother of yours was dead and is alive again; he was lost and is found.'"

In this story, also referred to as the story of the prodigal son, the father grants the younger son his wish and gives him his entire share of the family inheritance. The younger of two sons takes his entire inheritance and squanders it on anything and everything. The net result being he loses all his money and is left with not even a morsel of food and he ends up eating food that was used to feed the swine.

The father in this story never gives up on looking for the return of his lost son. But the swine-food-eating son has to do it on his own. He needs to realize that he needs his father's help and must come back to his father for that help on his own accord. The proverbial ball is entirely in his court. The son in this story eventually does turn back to his father.

The father embraces the younger son when he finally finds his way home from having learned his lesson. The older brother in this story seems more than a little upset about the situation. He says, "I've been here all along, and how come you're celebrating when this good-for-nothing son of yours has come back [I paraphrase of course]." The father says something here that is often overlooked in the telling of this story, a statement that needs to be reiterated to everyone who goes on to explore the wild side of life.

GOD will forgive you of your sin in that the father embraces the son on his return and celebrates his return. It shows how loving and caring the father really is. But whatever happened to the consequences of his waywardness? The story depicts in a no small way that you will face the consequences of your choices. What does that mean? Isn't he forgiven? By all means he is forgiven by the father (against whom alone he has chosen to sin).

And here's the part that is often overlooked: if you would pay attention to the father's conversation to the older son (Luke 15:31-32) wherein you can see the father comforting the older son, you can visualize an older father gently talking with his son with all the love and care in his eyes. Just the looks alone would tell the older son this, "My son, I understand your concerns. Don't you worry. I am your father. Your brother was once lost, but now he is found. I want you to be happy for him." But if you zoom in a little further into this conversation, you will hear the father say, "You are always with me, and everything I have is yours." You see the one-half of all the father's wealth that would have belonged to the younger son has already been given out to him, and he chose to do whatever he did with it. The father is loving, but he is also just. He shows no signs of compromise. He waits for his son to come back to him on his very own, and he lets the older son know that even though he was throwing a big party for this younger son of his, even though he is truly excited about his return, he lets the older son know that his promise to him will not be shaken or altered or forgotten and that everything he owns now belongs to his older son and rightfully so. There's neither a compromise on the amount of the father's love toward HIS children nor a compromise on the amount of the Father's fairness toward HIS children.

The life lesson to all of GOD's children is this: GOD is all loving and all caring, but he is also all just and all fair. You can see this quality of GOD brilliantly displayed in the life of Moses. Let me draw your attention to the book of Numbers 14:6-25:

Then Moses and Aaron fell facedown in front of the whole Israelite assembly gathered there. [6] Joshua son of Nun and Caleb son of Jephunneh, who were among those who had explored the land, tore their clothes [7] and said to the entire Israelite assembly, "The land we passed through and explored is exceedingly good. [8] If the Lord is pleased with us, he will lead us into that land, a land flowing with milk and honey, and will give it to us. [9] Only do not rebel against the Lord. And do not be afraid of the people of the land, because we will swallow them up. Their protection is gone, but the Lord is with us. Do not be afraid of them."

[10] But the whole assembly talked about stoning them. Then the glory of the Lord appeared at the Tent of Meeting to all the Israelites. [11] The Lord said to Moses, "How long will these people treat me with contempt? How long will they refuse to believe in me,

in spite of all the miraculous signs I have performed among them? [12] I will strike them down with a plague and destroy them, but I will make you into a nation greater and stronger than they."

[13] Moses said to the Lord, "Then the Egyptians will hear about it! By your power you brought these people up from among them. [14] And they will tell the inhabitants of this land about it. They have already heard that you, O Lord, are with these people and that you, O Lord, have been seen face to face, that your cloud stays over them, and that you go before them in a pillar of cloud by day and a pillar of fire by night. [15] If you put these people to death all at one time, the nations who have heard this report about you will say, [16] 'The Lord was not able to bring these people into the land he promised them on oath; so he slaughtered them in the desert.'

[17] "Now may the Lord's strength be displayed, just as you have declared: [18] 'The Lord is slow to anger, abounding in love and forgiving sin and rebellion. Yet

he does not leave the guilty unpunished; he punishes the children for the sin of the fathers to the third and fourth generation.' [19] In accordance with your great love, forgive the sin of these people, just as you have pardoned them from the time they left Egypt until now."

[20] The Lord replied, "I have forgiven them, as you asked. [21] Nevertheless, as surely as I live and as surely as the glory of the Lord fills the whole earth, [22] not one of the men who saw my glory and the miraculous signs I performed in Egypt and in the desert but who disobeyed me and tested me ten times—[23] not one of them will ever see the land I promised on oath to their forefathers. No one who has treated me with contempt will ever see it. [24]But because my servant Caleb has a different spirit and follows me wholeheartedly, I will bring him into the land he went to, and his descendants will inherit it." [25]

The LORD expresses (in verse 12 of chapter 14) frustration over the lack of faith of the Israelites. HE says, "I will give them a terrible sickness and get rid of them," and then Moses begins to plead with GOD (verse 19) and asks GOD to forgive the children of Israel with an elaborate and deductive reasoning. GOD listens to Moses and says (in verse 20), "I have forgiven them as you asked." If this somehow makes you think that Moses and the rest of the Israelites can now breathe a sigh of relief, I implore you to think otherwise. Listen and observe as GOD speaks to Moses in verse 35. You will notice that while they were forgiven, the (earthly) consequences to their lack of faith can be clearly seen. After having witnessed all of God's glorious and mighty miracles, they (I don't know how) chose not to trust HIM for the entirety of their journey. So they faced the consequence of their actions. I am saying that on this side of heaven, we are bound to face the consequence of our actions. Sure GOD forgives our sins, and by his grace we are saved, but the consequences of some of our sins certainly have a way of catching up with us down here. So it was with that generation of Israelites that they all perished in the wilderness.

Allow me to interject and say, all that is expected of us for life and godliness is to simply trust and to simply have faith in the providence of our Almighty GOD and creator, the LORD JESUS CHRIST. Even if you are a responsible parent, I urge you to simply trust GOD with the lives of your children. As children reach the age of accountability, when they can distinguish right from wrong and they choose to do that which is right, they enjoy the complete benefit and the fulfillment of doing that right thing. Just like the prodigal son, if after all the love and affection and the proper upbringing, they choose not the narrow way. Are you to blame? Are you to sit on the corner of your house and keep worrying? I propose to you that the GOD who made the heavens and the earth cares more deeply for them than you ever can or will. So here's my question, where's the need to worry then? You say huh! What? Not just regarding children (I only use children as an example because they are very precious to you), but regarding anything and everything. Listen, live your life as a parent, as a brother, as a sister, as a teacher, as a leader, etc.; and learn to face the world with no worries. What can your worrying do? JESUS was right when he said in Matthew 6:25-34:

25 "Therefore I tell you, do not worry about your life, what you will eat or drink; or about your body, what you will wear. Is not life more important than food, and the body more important than clothes? 26 Look at the birds of the air; they do not sow or reap or store away in barns, and yet your heavenly Father feeds them. Are you not much more valuable than they? 27 Who of you by worrying can add a single hour to his life?

28 "And why do you worry about clothes? See how the lilies of the field grow. They do not labor or spin. 29 Yet I tell you that not even Solomon in all his splendor was dressed like one of these. 30 If that is how God clothes the grass of the field, which is here today and tomorrow is thrown into the fire, will he not much more clothe you, O you of little faith? 31 So do not worry, saying, 'What shall we eat?' or 'What shall we drink?' or 'What shall we wear?' 32 For the pagans run after all these things, and your heavenly Father knows that you need them. 33 But seek first his kingdom and

his righteousness, and all these things will be given to you as well. [34] Therefore do not worry about tomorrow, for tomorrow will worry about itself. Each day has enough trouble of its own."

Since I started by addressing the parents, if your child is showing signs of wandering away from the faith, I would like for you to do two things:

1. Pray for your children.

   James 5:16: "The effectual fervent prayer of a righteous man availeth much."

   Besides all the instruction and the education that you can somehow impart to your children, pray for them and lift them up to GOD ALMIGHTY. And He will lift the burden off your shoulders and directly intervene in helping raise that child. And you will see the divine interference in that HE will do a much better job of raising that child than you ever thought possible. Even as your child hears you and sees you praying for him or her, day in and day out, he or she is bound to have a difference in their lives and turn their life around.

2. Pray for yourselves.

You see GOD has a special purpose and a special plan for your life. That plan and that purpose must come to fruition, for his glory and for his praise. You're worrying and not trusting every aspect of your life to your Savior (including but not limited to raising children) will only slow you down. So much so that true happiness and true fulfillment will always be out of reach. So pray yourselves.

And pray this specific prayer, "GOD please help me live my life without any worries or concerns. I want to be at my very best for you. Let nothing or no one come in between you and me. Fill me with your SPIRIT that I may always bring you glory and honor. For me to live is CHRIST, and to die is gain. Be near me, guide me, and never leave me or forsake me. I am now and will always be yours and yours alone." In the mighty name of JESUS. Amen.

And HE will ever so gently reply to you—with words that will fill your heart and your soul, with words that will make every hair on your back stand up, with words that will reign in meaning and purpose and drive. And you will feel the much-needed assurance every day and every hour of your life, and you'll know beyond a shadow of a doubt that this is the CHRIST, the Holy one of Israel, and his words to you will be ever so true. It will be truer than the shining stars. It will be truer than the changing seasons. It will be truer than the morning dew. It will be truer than a mother's love. It will be truer than a father's discipline. It will be truer than a doting lover. It will be truer than a lover's embrace. It will be truer than a friend in need. It will be truer than a child's innocence. It will be truer than a Sunday sermon. It will be truer than the roaring oceans. It will be truer than the howling wind. It will be truer than any truths that you've ever known. You can't deny it. You can't explain it away. You can't repudiate it. You can't count it as nothing. The only thing you can do is to accept it, is to believe it, is to trust it, is to experience it, and to let it become real to you.

Such is the strength and the vigor and the glory and the power and the awe-inspiring nature of his promise. And here is HIS promise in all its glory, in all its truth, in all its vitality, in all its strength, boldly declaring as one promise for all times, for all mankind, once and for all:

And Lo I will be with you always, even until the end of this age.

Amen and amen and amen, and again I say, amen.
Praise the living GOD.

A Study Guide

Always with You

A Study Guide

T his study guide is designed for a small-group setting. I recommend that you form a small group in your local church (if you already don't have one). Predetermine the time and place where this would take place. The discussion time should last anywhere between one hour to one and half hour. Arrange for the people to arrive fifteen to twenty minutes ahead of time and allow some time for fellowshipping and some friendly banter. The host provides the room, the couches or chairs, and a dining table or a coffee table. I recommend that the members of the small group bring some form of refreshments, and as they arrive, they could be directed to the dining table or a large enough table to place their refreshments. This kind of small groups creates an abundance of great kinship. You get to know one another, and the time you spend together has far-reaching benefits than you ever imagined possible. I am giving detailed instructions just so you get to know the type of setup needed to encourage a meaningful small-group time. Please feel free to tailor-make this group setting that best suits your small-group church setting.

The host should go over the material ahead of time and prepare oneself to have a quality small-group ministry. It's a great privilege to be a host. You can even rotate the meeting place every week (if the situation so warrants) so long as it does not have any adverse effect on things such as travel time, parking time, and any other inconveniences. If you are the host, do not make a big deal if someone missed a meeting (although I highly discourage missing a session). Encourage them to the best of your ability so they can feel comfortable enough to participate. And the discussion times are designed specifically to create action plans that will benefit both the local church and Christendom in general.

If you have already purchased the book, the study guide comes free of cost along with the book. You could also purchase just the study guide by itself or the DVD and/or the MP3 version of the book from our website. Once again, if you follow the study guide as a weekly study for your small-group setting, you will have ample time to respond and follow through to your GOD-given goals.

This study guide is designed to encourage your faith and challenge your faith. It will also help you become an active participant of your local church and the community at large. Above all, getting involved in the Gospel ministry of JESUS CHRIST is what this is all about. May GOD bless your efforts.

The study guide is also designed to foster personal growth. Both the host and the participants will find themselves nourished by the richness of their discussion and the challenges that ensue.

It is my prayer that GOD richly pour out his HOLY SPIRIT on all your discussion times and that you will sincerely follow through everything that the HOLY SPIRIT prompts you to do. And above all, bring glory and honor to our LORD JESUS CHRIST and be thoroughly and completely blessed by this effort.

Chapter Outline

Chapter 1

1. HIS word is _____, HIS word is _____, HIS word is alive, and above all, it is sufficient to meet your _____ need. If ever you needed an affirmation, if you ever needed an encouragement or a shoulder to cry on, you can find the _____ you need in HIS _____ words.

2. No one's _____ and walk is the same as the other, yet there are always some _____ elements that seem to draw us closer to one another and therein allow us to see in each of us the indwelling of the _____.

3. We always have the _____. The choice is between having _____ in GOD and choosing to give HIM credit or choosing to believe in _____ or coincidence or even mere _____.

4. *"And* Lo I will be with you always, even until the end of this age."

Vocabulary Help

strong, true, every, strength, precious, experience, common,

ALMIGHTY, choice, faith, chance, luck, and

A Time to Discuss

1. Where did you grow up (state, city, etc.), and what's unique about where you were born? People thought nothing important ever would happen in Bethlehem. But it did. What happened there changed history. Yours and mine. In the light of this, what uniqueness can you remember about where you were born and where you grew up?

2. Can you describe your faith during your growing-up years?

3. When did you first realize the existence of an Almighty God in your life? What events surrounded your realization?

4. Can you name one incident in your life where you clearly felt the hand of GOD intervening in the events of your life? What did you do?

5. When were you able to distinguish between chance or circumstantial occurrence or mere luck to an overwhelming "Yes, it is the hand of GOD" (faith that is)?

6. Whom do you consider most influential in your walk with GOD?

7. Are you still searching, or can you say with certainty that there is a GOD above and HIS name is JESUS and HE cares about all the details of your life?

Chapter Outline

Chapter 2

1. GOD is so meticulously and thoroughly _____ the events of a Christian's life with a _____ that far surpasses any human profession or endeavor.

2. If life is to be enjoyed, there is only one way to do it. It is by having the _____ that the hand of the Almighty is at work in your life and that he has _____ to be there for you all the way to the end.

3. "And _____ I will be with you always, even until the end of this age."

4. Amen.

orchestrating, precision, knowledge, promised, to

Vocabulary Help

A Time to Discuss

1. Did you know that you are in ministry whether or not anyone gave you a title? It's called the priesthood of the believer. What does that mean to you? And in the light of this information, if somebody were to ask you if you are in ministry, what would your answer be? And how would knowing this make your life any different.

2. What qualities do you think JESUS expects a believer/minister to have?

3. What qualities are you missing? Do you have the time? How much time does ministry take? Are you in a secular job? Can you still be doing ministry even if you were not a paid staff in the church?

4. Ministry is often an extension of your relationship with JESUS CHRIST. And as such, name just a few ways by which that extension can be put to use in your local church body.

5. A ministry partner is any person whom the LORD JESUS CHRIST has led your way to help you along in your ministerial tasks. Before you consider a ministry partner, what are some tasks of yours that you consider ministry tasks?

Chapter Outline

Chapter 3

1. Genesis 17:17

   Abraham bowed face down on the ground and

   _____ and he said to himself, "Can a man have a

   child when he is a _____ years old? Can Sarah give

   birth when she is _____?"

2. He understands that GOD can do anything, but

   _____ tells him that the times for _____ great

   things are up.

3. GOD can and will do anything that is needed to accomplish HIS _____ and _____.

4. "And Lo _____ will be with you always, even until the end of this age."

Amen.

will purpose, I

Laughed, hundred, ninety, pragmatism, accomplishing

Vocabulary Help

A Time to Discuss

1. Did you know that you can accomplish great things for JESUS CHRIST no matter what your age? If so, tell the group what are some of the things that you want to accomplish for GOD ALMIGHTY. (You don't have to tell them your age!)

2. Who does GOD call to do HIS mighty work for HIM?

3. What work do you consider mighty? And why? (Discuss with the group.)

4. Have you ever tried to help GOD fulfill HIS promise in your life? What happened? Trying to help GOD to help us is a very natural instinct (even Abraham did it), but faith dictates that we overcome that natural instinct. What character trait must we build in order that we might be able to overcome that natural instinct? Can a sincere prayer be a starting point for the building up of such character traits? Take some time and pray for one another in your group.

Chapter Outline

Chapter 4

1. _____: "to see someone step forward and bless another person's life" (it is nothing short of divine).

2. The GOD of the _____ is a caring GOD, and the salvation of his people is important to _____, even if it is only one _____ soul out in the middle of _____. HE is still willing and able to bend _____ to reach that one soul.

3. If GOD can care _____ to go over (what may seem like) the small details of life so exquisitely, how much

more do you think does he care about _____ life and
_____ well-being. The answer is more than you'll
ever know.

4. This pattern of trust slowly becomes so _____ that
when the person is physically absent, he or she elicits the
_____ amount of trust from you.

5. HIS physical absence or otherwise called HIS _____
absence is what is causing many to question the different
_____ of GOD.

6. The very knowledge that there is a GOD who is in
_____, that there is a GOD who is in charge causes
a wellspring of hope to arise in you. The outpouring of
that wellspring is what we call _____, and this causes
many doors and windows of _____ to come your
way, and life as you know it will _____ be the same
again.

7. The faith journey that you begin is never a _____
journey or a journey of _____

8. "And Lo I _____ be with you always, even until the end of this age."

9. Amen.

Vocabulary Help

generosity, universe, HIM, lonely, nowhere, heaven, earth, your, your, pervasive, same, optical, attributes, control, faith, opportunities, never, lonely, solitude, will

A Time to Discuss

1. Describe briefly a meaningful relationship that you have, and tell the group in your own words what it took to make that relationship meaningful.

2. Share a moment in time when you needed help and a total stranger came forward to help you. What was the first thought that crossed your mind? Why?

3. In the Bible story did you think the Ethiopian eunuch deserved that kind of attention from GOD Almighty? What about your own life? Are there areas in your life that you think is probably too much or too little for GOD to care about?

4. What life lesson can we learn from Ethiopian eunuch's story in terms of what we deserve?

5. Trusting in JESUS CHRIST does not require elaborate rituals. It does not require any religion and does not require a rite of passage or any such. It only requires a relationship established on the basis of faith. A simple trust if you will. Have you found your ability to trust as a very simple process, or are you struggling to establish a trust of any kind simple or otherwise? Is a simple trust really simple as far as you are concerned? Share with the group. Pray for three specific people within your sphere of influence that they may experience this simple faith in JESUS CHRIST.

Chapter Outline

Chapter 5

1. _____ at all levels is good, but the _____ of any type of reconciliation needs to be carefully thought through.

2. Whatever his choice, he had a _____ audience eagerly peering through the reasoning skills of the _____

3. Both the believers and the nonbelievers alike often seem to make this comment in life, saying, "Oh! But GOD looks at the _____!" This is often an _____ mechanism.

4. A child must be raised in a _____, caring, and _____ home in order to help bring about any kind of

a good upbringing. It is indeed pivotal to have a strong

_____.

5. Unlike your earthly father, GOD incarnate in JESUS CHRIST will not _____you or leave you or forsake you, no matter what the odds. When no one else was willing to stand up for that woman that day, JESUS did, and he still does when you place your _____ in HIM.

6. HE is and always will be our ever-_____ help and our strong _____.

7. "And Lo I will _____ with you always, even until the end of this age."

8. Amen.

nurturing, foundation, abandon, trust, present, tower, be reconciliation, modality, captive, Almighty, heart, escape, loving

Vocabulary Help

A Time to Discuss

1. What are some ways as a church you can help minister to someone who has gone through or is going through some sort of abandonment issues?

2. How can you, in a small group setting, be more receptive in identifying and ministering to these individuals with some abandonment issues? (They are not going to come and spell it out to you and say, "Hey, I have some abandonment issues!)

3. Church does not mean a building although we go to one. Church does not mean a set way of doing things. It simply means us, the people of GOD the LORD JESUS CHRIST. If "we" are the church, then why is it important to identify a need within the church? What are some ways you can be an effective minister of the Gospel by identifying the needs within a church?

4. In what ways can we broaden what we see as an individual need to what we see as a corporate need and a community need? How can your local church be involved in this endeavor?

5. Plan within your small group five action plans. That will identify a need in your community and five ways by which you can meet that need as a small group.

6. Here's a bonus question: what do you think JESUS wrote on the sand when everyone were busy yelling and screaming at the woman caught in the act of adultery?

Chapter Outline

Chapter 6

1. The GOD who knit you in your mother's womb, the GOD who knows all the days of your life even before one of them comes to be has also _____ and _____ everything you will ever need to face this moment in time.

2. vv5 One who was there had been an _____ for thirty-eight years. vv6 When Jesus saw him lying there and learned that he had been in this condition for a _____ time, he asked him, "Do you want to get _____?"

3. vv14 Later Jesus found him at the temple and said to him, "See, you are well again. _____ sinning or something _____ may happen to you." vv15 The man went away and told the Jews that it was _____ who had made him well.

4. GOD takes HIS time. HE _____ and _____ orchestrates everything for the good of HIS children. HE does not _____, none whatsoever.

5. Our job is to simply trust his _____. Because, at the end of the day, it would not matter what anybody said or did, so long as you had an _____ with JESUS the Christ and you were _____.

6. Faith and _____ alone will draw you closer to your maker.

7. Whether it be a _____ man by a pool near Bethesda two thousand years ago or whether it be Abraham or Moses or Gideon or David or any of the biblical characters, they all had to wait until it was time for GOD Almighty to work in their lives. Surprisingly, what was

_____ for Abraham and Moses and David is also true for _____.

8. "And Lo I will be _____ you always, even until the end of this age."

Vocabulary Help

JESUS, worse, stop, well, long, invalid, predestined, prearranged, faith, healed, encounter, timing, waver, methodically, carefully, crippled, true, you, with

| A Time to Discuss |

1. What can we infer from Jessica's childhood? Do you know anyone in your group or otherwise who has lost a parent at a very young age? GOD always has a special eye on the fatherless (or the motherless or the orphaned), and in the light of this, can you can see how your church can make a tremendous influence/difference in their lives and allow them to see the hand of GOD at work in their life? Find at least three unique ways by which you can make a difference in their life?

2. (John 15:14: Later Jesus found him at the temple and said to him, "See, you are well again. Stop sinning or something worse may happen to you.") What do think JESUS meant by this? What was the focus of JESUS's statement in this verse?

3. GOD is always working in making us more into the image of HIS son, JESUS CHRIST, which means we must change by nature and character. What character trait do you think is GOD working on when he seems like HE hasn't answered your prayer yet?

4. What in your opinion is simple faith? Does having faith in GOD mean losing control over your life?

5. Can you name two ways by which you can help a fellow Christian brother or sister grow in their faith?

6. What is Jessica doing by the end of this story while she is waiting on the LORD JESUS? What spiritual truth can we learn about waiting on the LORD from her experience?

Chapter Outline

Chapter 7

1. Isaiah: 53: Vv2 He grew up before him like a tender shoot
    and like a root out of dry ground. He had no _____ or
    _____ to attract us to him, _____ in his appearance
    that we should desire him.

    vv3 He was _____ and _____ by men, a man
    of sorrows, and familiar with suffering. Like one from
    whom men _____ their faces he was despised, and we
    _____ him not.

2. If anyone could have made himself extremely _____
    (by virtue of the definition of external beauty), it was

JESUS, but he lived in such a way to show that what really matters is on the _____.

3. Each and every one of us must decide to make a _____ to become a positive _____ in someone else's life.

4. *Philippians 4:13: I can do all things through _____ which strengthened me.

5. Everyone needs a daily _____, a daily _____, a daily building up—that sort of a help can only be gotten from our ever-present help—our savior JESUS CHRIST.

6. "And Lo I will be with _____ always, even until the end of this age."

Vocabulary Help

beauty, majesty, nothing, despised, rejected, hide, esteemed, attractive, inside, contribution, influence, CHRIST, strengthening, assurance, you

A Time to Discuss

1. How much importance do you give to external looks? What need or needs are we meeting or trying to meet through these efforts?

2. Where do you draw the line between "I won't comb my hair or wear any makeup ever!" to "I need a one hundred thousand dollar face-lift"? And how have you gone about it?

3. Consider Isaiah 53:2-3.

2 He grew up before him like a tender shoot and like a root out of dry ground. He had no beauty or majesty to attract us to him, nothing in his appearance that we should desire him. 3 He was despised and rejected by men, a man of sorrows, and familiar with suffering. Like one from whom men hide their faces he was despised, and we esteemed him not.

What do you picture of the image of JESUS as you read this passage?

4. What are some ways to improve on the self-esteem of a brother or sister; and how can you, either individually or as a group, contribute to the active building of one another's self-esteem?

5. Write down (for your personal growth) names of five people and come up with an active action plan on how you can make a positive difference in the lives of these individuals.

6. Here's a question to ponder: why was it important for JESUS to be born in a manger and live homeless? And as Isaiah says, "*Nothing in his appearance* that we should desire him." Nothing! Nothing in his appearance to be desired for! Why? Maybe he was telling you, telling me, telling us something!

7. What can we infer from Jessica's childhood? Do you know anyone in your group or otherwise who has lost a parent at a very young age? GOD always has a special eye on the fatherless (or the motherless or the orphaned), and

in the light of this, can you can see how your church can make a tremendous influence/difference in their lives and allow them to see the hand of GOD at work in their life? Find at least three unique ways by which you can make a difference in their life?

8. (John 15:14: Later Jesus found him at the temple and said to him, "See, you are well again. Stop sinning or something worse may happen to you.") What do think JESUS meant by this? What was the focus of Jesus' statement in this verse?

9. GOD is always working in making us more into the image of HIS son, JESUS CHRIST, which means we must change by nature and character. What character trait do you think is GOD working on when he seems like HE hasn't answered your prayer yet?

10. What in your opinion is simple faith? Does having faith in GOD mean losing control over your life?

11. Can you name two ways by which you can help a fellow Christian brother or sister grow in their faith?

12. What is Jessica doing by the end of this story while she is waiting on the LORD JESUS? What spiritual truth can we learn about waiting on the LORD from her experience?

Chapter Outline

Chapter 8

1. He who _____ a good work in you will be _____ to complete it.

2. 1 Samuel 1:7-8: This went on year after year. Whenever Hannah went up to the house of the Lord, her rival *provoked* her till she _____ and would not *eat*. 8 Elkanah her husband would say to her, "Hannah, why are you weeping? Why don't you eat? Why are you _____? Don't I mean more to you than ten sons?"

3. Imagine, if Hannah was told in the midst of all her problems that she shouldn't *worry* and that she should

simply _____ GOD and that GOD was going to bless her immensely beyond her wildest _____, Hannah could have done one of two things, either she trusted that _____ and waited _____ or she could have taken an inventory of her life and circumstances and _____ that nothing great was ever going to happen to her.

4. No matter _____ you find yourself in life, God can _____ great things in your life, if you will only _____ Him.

5. "And Lo I will be with you _____, even until the end of this age."

6. All you need to _____ is that his presence is _____ with you.

Vocabulary Help

began, faithful, provoked, wept, eat, downhearted, worry, trust, imaginations, encouragement, patiently, concluded, where, accomplish, remember, always, always

A Time to Discuss

1. What life lessons can we glean from Nevena's life experiences?

2. The tenacity of Nevena the Olympian is somewhat analogous to the tenacity of Hannah, the mother of Samuel, in that they were both hopeful that the GOD of Israel, the LORD JESUS CHRIST, will deliver them from their troubles. What Bible character do you most identify with? And why?

3. What support network did Hannah have to help her through her struggles? What support network do you have to help you along life's journey? Are you part of your local church's support network? If yes, then how can you make that support network better? If no, then why not?

4. Why did Hannah refuse to be comforted by her husband Elkanah? Briefly describe what life lesson can be gleaned from this conduct of Hannah.

5. Name three ways by which we can comfort the Hannahs of this world.

Chapter Outline

Chapter 9

1. Oftentimes, we perceive what the problems are (to varying degrees of course), and there arises a deep _____, a _____ if you will, to get up and do something about it. But _____? The question of _____ to most of its perceived problems is simply "what can I do" or "I _____ know what to do."

2. Often, the first step is to _____ that which is wrong as clearly as possible.

3. The second step is not to go along with that which is _____, immaterial of the _____. (Trust the Almighty to deliver.)

4. Faith must be accompanied by _____.

5. You will find several _____ come across your path in life, and in each one of those paths, you will be given the _____ either to do something about it or to simply stand on the _____ and wonder as to what could have been or should have been.

6. Don't lose your place in history by being _____and don't lose the opportunity to make a _____ (no matter how small).

7. "And Lo I will be with you always, _____ until the end of this age."

Vocabulary Help

longing groaning, what humanity don't identify, wrong

consequences, works, hurdles, opportunity shorelines, complacent,

difference, even

A Time to Discuss

1. Put yourself in the shoes of Shadrach, Meshach, and Abednego and honestly answer (to yourself) if under the same circumstances would you have taken a trip to the (inferno) furnace. If you said yes, you have nothing to boast about because that kind of faith isn't a "see what I can do" faith. If you said no, you are not a bad Christian because of it. The reality is the ones who can enter the furnace and the ones outside both have the need for a savior. And JESUS is the savior of both. And here's my question: what then is the purpose of the furnace experience? Discuss.

2. What is the role of a Christian in the matters of social justice? When do we stand up and raise our voices in unison, and when do we not? What is our primary focus in each of these situations?

Food for Thought

When Christian missionaries are sent around the world by mission agencies, they are often instructed not to interfere with the rule of law (no matter how harsh) of the local government. The primary task is to simply learn to lean on JESUS as the author and finisher of our faith and continue to believe that even in the harshest of conditions, when you see injustice, be reminded that our war isn't against the powers and principalities of this world.

3. The world responds to who you appear to be externally. GOD responds to who you appear to be internally. True or false? If your answer is true, then how is a large-scale change brought about? If your answer is false, then go see your pastor.

4. What problem predominantly dominates your community? What are some ways by which you can respond to this crisis as a church? Name three ways by which you can respond as an individual or as a group. Help your church in meeting this crisis.

5. How do you perceive the timing of GOD in the case of delivering Shadrach, Meshach, and Abednego? Was GOD late or was GOD on time or was GOD early? In

your own life, briefly share if you're in the furnace yet or not. Can you feel the heat yet? How do you perceive GOD's timing is in your life?

Chapter Outline

Chapter 10

1. Imagine if _____ had a call-in radio show. What would you want to call in about?

2. First of all, it would be the _____ show on earth.

3. Second of all, even though the number of callers would be _____high, somehow the lines would never be too busy for anybody. _____ and _____ would both get the same treatment.

4. Third of all, it would be a _____ show. Anybody from anywhere can call in and speak in their own language

(there will be no special signage with a "se habla español" needed!), and expect to be understood _____.

5. The only thing you need to have is _____. Call on HIM with faith today and see what marvelous things he can show you or _____ through you (Jeremiah 33:1-3).

6. HE not only hears you, but HE also _____ for you, so much that HE never will leave you or _____ you. I hope you can tune your ears today and hear *HIM*.

7. "And Lo I will be with you always, even _____ the end of this age."

Vocabulary Help

JESUS, what hottest, immensely princes, paupers, multilingual perfectly, faith, accomplish, cares, forsake, HIM, until

| A Time to Discuss |

1. In what ways can you improve your individual prayer time? Name two ways by which you can improve individual prayer times.

2. In what ways can you improve corporate prayer times? Name two ways by which you can improve corporate prayer times.

3. If GOD knows all your thoughts and deeds and actions, then why is it important to communicate (through prayer) to him about some of the things or all of the things that are happening in your lives?

4. JESUS taught us how to pray. What principle? If any from this how-to are you using on a daily basis, and why?

5. What has been your biggest barrier in having an effective prayer life? Name at least one barrier. As a group, pause and pray for GOD to intervene in this one area.

Chapter Outline

Chapter 11

1. *God's* voice is also heard by those who know HIM. He doesn't make a _____ sound, but rather he calls us by name.

2. The success of your life isn't based on your _____ to hear HIS voice, but rather it's based on how you choose to respond to what you've heard. Remember Judas had heard just as much as the other apostles, all firsthand information, yet he chose to go the way of _____. Something to consider!

3. As human beings we all have the inherent need for
_____. Letting me know that things are going to be
taken care of by someone who loves me and cares for me
and who has _____ to follow through on all their
promises makes living life with *passion* so much more
possible.

4. Abundant life isn't a _____ but a journey. Don't
keep asking the question "are we _____ yet" and
miss out on the journey.

5. Life isn't lived in years at a time or _____ at a time
but rather a *day* at a time.

6. "And Lo I will be with you always, even until _____ of
this age."

passion, destination, there, decades, day, the end.

God's, generic, capability, perdition, certainty, wherewithal

Vocabulary Help

208

A Time to Discuss

1. What are some ways by which people obtain certainty in life? In what way do you obtain certainty in life?

2. If uncertainty leads you to worry and if JESUS CHRIST asked you not to worry, what then is there to do with uncertainty?

3. Make a list of worries, worries that concern you the most (a top ten if you will). Now

   a. pray earnestly about each one of them a committed and consistent prayer for each one of them,

   b. remove yourself out of the equation, and pray with the same amount of intensity that you prayed for yourself, with the same amount of commitment and with the same amount of consistency (if not more), and pray for your neighbor.

4. Create a small fun play to remember this day as an Ebenezer, a remembrance if you will (e.g., who has the

loudest burp, who can hold their breath the longest, etc.) to help you know that in this place you sincerely and earnestly prayed to give to the LORD JESUS CHRIST all of your worries, and pray together as a group and that from this day forward you will claim all your certainties from knowing the savior and in what he can do for you.

Chapter Outline

Chapter 12

1. The life and story of any of the Old Testament _____,
   whether it be Daniel, Ezekiel, or Jeremiah—the pattern
   you'll notice in the lives of each of these individuals is
   that they were all _____ of their times. They were
   never men who went with the flow. If anything they went
   _____ the flow.

2. The Old Testament prophets were inevitably led of GOD,
   and what they said and did still remains _____ to our
   lives. Their _____ yielded them names such as weird,
   crazy, etc.; but they irrevocably remained an anachronism

of their era. But what they said and did about 1,500 (or so) years ago still stands the test of _____.

3. GOD cared about every _____ of the temple, and we know from the New Testament that GOD's SPIRIT no longer _____ in the handmade temples anymore, but he resides in the human heart. GOD is the same yesterday, today, and forever; and as such, He cares about all the _____ of your life.

4. We all need to hear _____ from time to time. It doesn't matter how much you know because these affirmations become the building blocks that build you from the inside out. It seems like the distance from the ear to the _____ is shorter than the distance from the _____ to the heart.

5. The GOD who cares about the details of your life—by that I mean all the details of your life—has _____ by witnesses such as Abraham, Moses, Elijah, and Enoch that HE is and will always be our _____. He provides, abundantly more than you've ever _____ possible.

6. "And Lo I will be with you always, even until the end _____ age."

Vocabulary Help

prophets, trailblazers, against, pertinent, sacrifices, time, aspect, resides, details, affirmations, heart, brain, testified, provider, imagined, of this

A Time to Discuss

1. What life lesson can we learn from Brother Bill's life story?

2. Why was it necessary for Brother Bill to hear encouragements, things he knew about GOD all along? What can we learn from this?

3. Can you describe a Sunday Christian? What measures can you take to avoid being a Sunday Christian? Name three measurable ways for your own life that would help you stay a Christian at all times.

4. Why was GOD so specific about all the details of how the temple was to be built? (Food for thought: Have you noticed how nobody during that time asked GOD why?

"Why do you have to be so specific, GOD?" Simply because HE is GOD, and we don't ask HIM why or what or where or when? The answer will always be HE will in HIS time, in HIS way, to anyone, anywhere in any way HE chooses, and for any reason. I think you get the picture, but I believe as a group, it's good to ponder these things; and I have learned so much more in a group setting than doing my own private study.)

5. Write down names of five different people whom you find very difficult to get along with. In the light of Philippians 4:8, write next to each name a true thing, a noble thing, a lovely thing, a virtuous thing, and a praiseworthy thing; and begin praying to GOD to heal and mend that broken relationship.

Chapter Outline

Chapter 13

1. The level of your _____ (about your children's eating habits) isn't directly _____ to the results that produce a healthy eating habit in a growing child's life.

2. There's no medal in _____ or on earth given out to those who _____ or got _____ out the most.

3. Luke 15: 31-32 "'My son,' the father said, 'you are always with me, and _____ I have is yours. But we had to celebrate and be glad, because this brother of yours was *dead* and is alive again; he was *lost* and is _____.'"

4. The prodigal son _____ to realize that he needs his
   father's help and must come back to his father on his own
   _____. The proverbial ball was entirely in his court.
   The son in this story _____ does turn back to his
   father.

5. The story depicts in a no small way that you will face the
   _____ of your *choices*.

6. GOD is all _____ and all caring, but he is also all
   _____ and all fair.

7. Live your life as a parent, as a brother, as a sister, as a
   teacher, as a leader, etc.; and learn to face the world with
   no *worries*. What can your _____ do? JESUS was right
   when he said in Mathew 6:25-34, "Therefore I tell you,
   do not worry about your life, what you will eat or drink;
   or about your body, what you will wear. Is not life more
   important than food, and the body more _____ than
   clothes?"

8. "And Lo I will be with you always, even until the end of
   this _____."

just, worries, worrying, important, age
lost, found, needed, accord, eventually, consequences, choices, loving,
worries, proportional, heaven, worried, stressed, everything, dead

Vocabulary Help

A Time to Discuss

1. What is the correlation between worrying and problem solving?

2. When it comes to problem solving and the problems are our own children, what godly approach should we defer to? If it takes a village to raise a kid, in what ways can a local church be the village to a growing child?

3. Parents must learn to relinquish control; the more a child is involved in the spiritual matters of the church, the easier it will be to relinquish control. Determine five different ways by which you can deliberately relinquish control to the growing child. Be deliberate in getting them involved in the church. Get godly counsel and help; seek out extra help in those areas where you are weak.

4. Discuss the story of the prodigal son. Take turns among the group with each one playing the role of a father, the role of the older son, and the role of the younger son; and then switch places and repeat. Discuss the story in these characters and try defending their point of view.

5. Is what is important to you important to GOD? Is what is important to GOD important to you?

Index

NOTES

NOTES

NOTES

NOTES

NOTES

NOTES